Jesus and Postmodernism

James Breech

Fortress Press   Minneapolis

Library of Congress Catalog Card Number 89-84944
ISBN 0-8006-2043-7

Printed in the United States of America

93   92   91   90   89   1   2   3   4   5   6   7   8   9   10
                                                      AF1-2043

For my sons
Matthew David Breech
and
Lylford Donne Breech

Contents

Foreword 7
Preface 11

CHAPTER 1

If Jesus Is the Answer, What Is the Question? 13

    From "God Is Dead" to "Death Is God" 15
    Anthropological Implications 17
    American Narcissism and Psychic Survivors 19
    What Has Jesus to Do with Postmodernism? 21
        What Counts as Evidence? 23
        The Task of Reconstruction 25
        The Gap in Jesus' Stories 27

CHAPTER 2

Narrative Decisions and Moral Choices 31

    Life Grounded in the Real 32
    The Sense of an Ending 34
        Closure as Useful Fiction 35
        Closure as Harmful Illusion 36
        Closure as Self-Accounting 38
    Closure in Ancient Storytelling 40
        Myths 41
        Legends and Anecdotes 45
        Fables 51
    Can One Narrativize without Moralizing? 53

CHAPTER 3
Did Jesus Tell True Stories?   57

    Bounded Time   57
    History and Fiction in the New Testament   59
        Jesus Told Fictions, Not Lies   60
        The Hermeneutical Problem   62
    Jesus and the Emancipation of Moral Imagination   64
        Conventional Narrative Authority   64
        Jesus' Narrative Authority   66
    Modes of Being Human in Time and Story   68
        Sequential Time   69
        The Core Phonodramatic Parables   69
        Motivation and Agency   70
        Multilinear Time and the Personal Mode   72
    Living in Unending Story   75

Notes   79

Index   93

Foreword

The 1905 term at the University of Strasbourg included a course by a young lecturer at work on studies about Jesus. His appointment had been contested within the faculty; his course did nothing to relieve the anxieties of senior colleagues. The lectures subjected a century's worth of scholarly research on Jesus to searching critique. The lesson to be drawn from the exercise was this:

> The historical Jesus of whom the criticism of the future will draw the portrait will not be a Jesus Christ to whom the religious of the present can ascribe according to long-cherished custom its own thoughts and ideas, as it did with the Jesus of its own making. Nor will this Jesus be a figure which can be made by a popular treatment to be sympathetic and universally intelligible to the multitude. The historical Jesus will be to our time a stranger and an enigma. He passes by our time, and returns to his own.

The young instructor was Albert Schweitzer; his lectures are known today as "The Quest of the Historical Jesus."

Since that time questing for the historical Jesus has gone on, and on, and on. Only now, however, are there signs and portents of a new age: the advent of "the criticism of the future" of which Schweitzer spoke. James Breech is its herald.

Breech is well known within the guild of New Testament scholars. There his work receives the only sort of respect that really counts—like it or not, no one dares ignore it. The reason is simple. This brand of biblical study is fresh, daring, and provocative, and all the more so because it is too exacting to be trendy. One example may suffice. Like a master sleuth who finds clues by noting something extraordinary about the ordinary, Breech capitalizes on decades of parable research by noting that the silences of Jesus are as telling as his words.

New findings of this order are Breech's stock-in-trade. They come as welcome news to those who want to know more about Jesus and as well-deserved jolts to those who assume they already know all there is about him. Our portraits of Jesus can never be quite the same after Breech is through with them. In any case, the Jesus who has been spied by this questor is too important to be left to historians of antiquity alone.

That conviction likely explains why Breech agreed to share his most recent thinking about Jesus with the audience of nonspecialists—faculty members, alumnae and alumni, Christian pastors and Christian laity, and any other interested parties— who attended the 1986 Earl Lectures at the Pacific School of Religion in Berkeley, California. It was certainly uppermost in the minds of those who invited him to address the gathering. The Earl Lectures were established, four years before Schweitzer lectured at Strasburg, by the generous act of a layman, Mr. Edwin T. Earl. They are dedicated to the proposition that critical inquiry and Christian commitment go hand in hand. It is a proposition that can never be taken for granted. Breech defends it by a challenge to inquiring critics and committed Christians alike: let Jesus be Jesus.

In *Jesus and Postmodernism* the telltale marks of Schweitzer's criticism of the future are everywhere in evidence. Breech insists that only by letting Jesus return to the past, his own past, do we gain a proper sense of his significance for the present, our own present. Precisely because he is "a stranger and an enigma" to our time, Jesus discloses a way of living and dying— a "mode of being human"—which comes as a surprise to us. To inquiring critics, Breech's point may be phrased this way: Nothing is more dated than an up-to-date Jesus. To committed Christians, it might be put like this: When Jesus becomes all too familiar, he is no longer an amazing grace.

No less a mark of the criticism of the future is the deft interplay of interpretative strategies at work in *Jesus and Postmodernism*. Schweitzer rode the wave of modern historical-critical method. Breech plots his course through the swirling currents of postmodern hermeneutics. Historical criticism gives him a boost: The "authentic" words of Jesus must be recovered from their canonical plots. But Breech is a historical critic with a difference. Theology of story, narrative analysis, semiotics, ideology-critique, philosophy after Heidegger and Wittgenstein— all these and more contribute to his quest.

The point of it all is by no means merely scholarly business as usual. Breech presses for the historical Jesus who still has a word to say to present-day inquirers, be they card-carrying Christians or not. This study takes up matters of consequence: "If Jesus Is the Answer, What Is the Question?"; "Narrative Decisions and Moral Choices"; "Did Jesus Tell True Stories?" The results of *Jesus and Postmodernism* are glimpses of Jesus which, like those of Albert Schweitzer in the olden days of modernity, are hazardous to the theological status quo. Voices cry, "lo here" and "lo there." Breech advises putting them all to the test. Is their Jesus a hostage to contemporaneity? This would be a counsel of despair were it not for the fact that Breech also suggests as our standard of judgment the world opened up by the "never-ending" stories told by Jesus. Since Jesus' never-ending stories open up a world far more near than we postmoderns realize, the Jesus who told them must be something *other* than what our popular theologians and a/theologians, as well as the moralists and antimoralists of the moment, have made of him. Not the least of Breech's services is to prompt second thoughts about what passes for gospel today.

One question remains. It is irrepressible. Does Breech himself produce a portrait of Jesus of his own postmodern making? The answer, of course, requires that we risk reading his text. Who knows, readers might be surprised.

James O. Duke
Professor of Church History
Pacific School of Religion

Preface

In my earlier work, historical-critical reconstruction and analysis of the authentic sayings and parables of Jesus led to the conclusion that, in response to humanity's religious questions, Jesus was silent. It was inevitable that questions would arise concerning the relevance of these sayings and parables for those of us living in the late twentieth century. I am grateful to Professor Doug Adams, to the Earl Lecture Committee, and to the Pacific School of Religion for providing me with the opportunity in 1986 to deal with these issues in a public forum through a series of lectures intended as a sequel to *The Silence of Jesus*. I much appreciated the receptiveness of the learned audience, and also the hospitality of everyone connected with the lecture program.

In this, the Preface to what is likely to be my last academic publication, I would like to state that I never intended to be a career academic, nor to make a career based on historical-Jesus research. Rather, my interest in joining the quest for the historical Jesus led me to acquire the tools of New Testament scholarship and to become a practicing scholar while engaged in the quest.

Having completed my quest for the historical Jesus, and having outlined what I believe to be its implications and relevance for today, I have been able to get on with my own life. The parables, after all, call one into the world.

I acknowledge the generous financial support of the Social Sciences and Humanities Research Council of Canada for my research, and thank the international community of scholars for their warm encouragement during the twenty-odd years when we were colleagues.

I am grateful to the following publishers for permission to quote from materials they have published:

Harcourt Brace Jovanovich, Orlando, Florida, for permission to quote from T.S. Eliot's "Murder in the Cathedral" and "Four Quartets" in *The Complete Poems and Plays* (copyright 1952).

Harvard University Press, Cambridge, Massachusetts, and the Loeb Classical Library for permissions to quote from

Ovid, *Metamorphoses*, 3d edition, revised by G.P. Gold (1977)
Seneca, *De Beneficiis*, trans. by John W. Basore (1935)
Lucian, *Toxaris or Friendship*, trans. by A.M. Harmon (1936)
Plato, *Phaedrus*, trans. by H.N. Fowler (1914)
Aristotle, *Rhetoric*, trans. by J.H. Fresse (1926)

Henry Holt and Company, New York, for permission to quote Robert Frost's "The Road Not Taken" and "Love and a Question" from *The Poetry of Robert Frost*, edited by Edward Connery Lathem (copyright 1916, 1934 by Holt, Rinehart and Winston and renewed 1944, 1962 by Robert Frost).

Socino Press, Ltd., London, for permission to quote from the "Ecclesiastes Rabbah" in *Midrash Rabbah*, edited by Freedman and Simon (copyright 1983).

I am happy that the distinguished Czech-born painter, Joseph Drapell, who now lives and paints in Toronto, has given his permission to display a reproduction of "New Direction" on the cover of *Jesus and Postmodernism*. His paintings, which are exhibited in major public, mainly North American, collections, including the Guggenheim and Boston's Museum of Fine Arts, utilize the techniques of contemporary painting without importing minimalist assumptions. I believe that his paintings express the deepest values of the Western tradition in a modern idiom.

Toronto   James Breech

1

If Jesus Is the Answer,
What Is the Question?

THE EVANGELICAL SLOGAN, "Jesus is the answer," expresses a conviction also held, though in a more sophisticated form, by all who understand themselves as Christians, for they believe that the tradition within which they live originated with Jesus of Nazareth.

Convinced that Jesus inaugurated a new reality, Christians have expressed their sense of this new reality by adopting and adapting patterns of life, and social and religious structures, from among those currently available. None of these patterns or structures was invented by Jesus. To give some examples: Neither the family nor the monastery was invented by Jesus, although those who understand themselves as Christian have utilized both of these structures to model social life. Even more radically, neither living morally nor being religious was invented by Jesus. Yet Christians have almost always believed that to follow his way involves adopting a moral, even religious, way of

13

life. Throughout its history, of course, the Christian tradition has been deeply bound up with culture.[1] And, from the beginnings of the Christian movement, theologians have found it necessary to evaluate critically the various patterns of life that Christians have chosen for expressing their understanding of what it means to live "in Christ." To take one example from the first generation of the Christian movement: When members of the church at Corinth began working miracles, speaking in tongues, and prophesying, as others both inside and outside the Christian movement had previously done, the apostle Paul questioned whether these patterns of religious behavior conformed to his sense of the truth of the gospel.

Can we, in our own day, identify specifically Christian attitudes towards reality and distinguish them from other, alien attitudes?[2] The German philosopher Max Scheler made just such an attempt. Calling Friedrich Nietzsche's discovery that *ressentiment* can be the source of value judgments "the most profound" among "the scanty discoveries which have been made in recent times about the origin of moral judgments," Scheler nevertheless argued that Nietzsche's characterization of Christian love as "the most delicate 'flower of *ressentiment*' " was mistaken.[3] Scheler's defense of Christian love depended on a series of distinctions between an allegedly specifically "Christian" system of value preferences and other, "alien," systems of value preference with which the "Christian" system had become confused: humanitarianism, altruism, egalitarianism, masochism.[4]

My concern in this volume is with the issues raised by contemporary efforts to portray the historical Jesus as thoroughly modern—or postmodern. There are today avant-garde theologians and New Testament scholars who have assimilated the assumptions of our postmodern condition[5] and who now proclaim a postmodernist gospel. How then does postmodernism manifest itself in theology?

From "God Is Dead" to "Death Is God"

THE MADMAN IN Nietzsche's *The Gay Science* announced that "God is dead." In my view, the modern period was characterized by the disintegration of the God of classical theism, whose final demise was celebrated by the death-of-God theologians of the late 1960s and 1970s. If the distinguishing mark of the modern period was the death of God, then the distinguishing mark of our period — that of postmodernism—is the conviction that death is God.

In the past, various persons and cultures have become preoccupied with the transience of all human endeavor. An awareness of human morality pervades The Epic of *Gilgamesh*, Homer's *Iliad*, the book of Ecclesiastes, Marcus Aurelius's *Meditations*, the view of the "friends of death" in the *Wisdom of Solomon*, the Anglo-Saxon poets, (the author of "The Seafarer," for example), Tennyson's *Idylls of the King*, and Freud's writings, to cite only a few examples from different times and places.

What is new and different in our situation today is the widespread sense that death is the reality which controls all life. Usually, this conviction remains at the level of unvoiced experience, but the self-proclaimed postmodernist a/theologian Mark C. Taylor articulates the idea explicitly:

> Postmodernism opens with the sense of irrecoverable loss and incurable fault. This world is infected by the overwhelming awareness of death — a death that "begins" with the death of God and "ends" with the death of our selves. We are in a time between times and a place which is no place.[6]

Taylor raises the ontological assumption, that death characterizes the real, to the level of a theological proposition; he announces that death is the primordial, inescapable reality that governs all existence. "God is death and death is absolute master."[7]

Postmodernist assumptions also underlie, though covertly,
the theology of the New Testament scholar John Dominic Crossan. His assumptions come nearest to the surface in *The Dark Interval.*[8] He takes his departure toward a "theology of limit" (13-
46) by invoking "our inevitable mortality" and by characteriz-
ing human life as "life-towards-death" (13, 14). Death is viewed
as the "failure" of life, for which one disciplines oneself by playing games, which he views as a "practice session . . . for life-
towards-death" (15-17). Playing games, particularly language
games, elicits the experience of "mortal jeopardy" (45, 122)
one feels when destruction threatens. This is "exciting" (45)
and "exhilarating" (40). Crossan describes our contemporary
condition with a recognizably postmodern image:

> There is no lighthouse keeper. There is no lighthouse.
> There is no dry land. There are only people living on rafts
> made from their own imaginations. And there is the sea.
> (44)

As in modernism, the lighthouse keeper, the God of classical
theism, has disappeared (41-42). Furthermore, as in postmodernism, the sea becomes the image for a potent force. The sea
moves about the rafts of the worlds we create from our imaginations, causes fissures in the rafts' structures, and breaks them
to pieces (44-45).

Crossan asks, "Why might it not be possible to experience
transcendence now from the call of the sea?" (44) The experience of having one's world broken by the sea is termed "transcendental experience" and "God . . . is the referrent of transcendental experience" (40). God, in other words, is "what we
experience in the *movement* of the raft, in the *breaks* in the raft's
structure, and above all, what can be experienced at the *edges*
of the raft itself" (45). In short, Crossan's theology of limits pro-
poses that the force which limits and subverts humanity's constructs is God. Here, dying is not merely the terminus of biolog-

ical life; destruction appears as a force that pervades all life as its ground and limit. Death is the ultimate reality—God.

Anthropological Implications

TAYLOR BOTH THOROUGHLY and explicitly develops the anthropology implied in the postmodern experience of the ultimacy of death. He states that the postmodern awareness of death begins with the death of God and ends with the death of the self, the logical and necessary consequence of the death of God.[9] Taylor proclaims that consenting to the mastery of death liberates one from the inhibitions of responsibility and conscience, thus enabling one to recover a "second innocence."[10] Taylor repudiates traditional values and advertises instead: the grotesque, careless, tasteless, foolish, aberrant, superficial, parasitic, nihilistic, patricidal, violent, scatological, infantile, cruel, and shameless, as well as profanity and perversion.[11] A life modeled on that of the prodigal son is recommended.[12]

In contrast to Taylor's, Crossan's stated goal is not the inversion of values.[13] His aim, apparently, is to relativize morality. His view, which is hardly novel, is that moral systems, like all "worlds," are spun from the human imagination, just as "a spider . . . weaves a web from inside itself and then dwells in it and calls it world."[14] He holds out the hope that making people aware of the subjective nature of their moral judgment will bring "freedom for human responsibility, personal and social decision, and the creation of those conventions which make us what we are."[15] Crossan believes that it is normal for people to expect the good to be rewarded and the bad to be punished. He argues that situations of reversal, in which supposedly "good" people give or do or receive "bad" things and "bad" people give or receive or do "good" things,[16] shatter our normal expectations[17] and hence "subvert our world."[18]

I rather doubt that many thinking adults would consider as world-shattering news the idea that reality does not fulfill our wishes. In any case, a more fundamental issue has to do with epistemology. According to Crossan, no language system can be seen as anything other than a game:

> Fundamentally, we find only what we need and see only what we want to see. We have no other possibility. Since the criterion of truth—correspondence with the external world—is absent, it is entirely a matter of indifference what opinions we adopt. All of them are equally true and equally false. And no one has the right to accuse anyone else of error.[19]

Those are not Crossan's words, but Freud's, who burlesques the position of "intellectual nihilists." Crossan's own summary of his position says something quite similar:

> I argued the proposition that we live in story like fish in the sea. It does not at all trouble me to contemplate the inevitability that this too must be a story, because it is the story in which I now have to live, and I know that in this I am not alone. I am quite aware that there are other master-stories around, and to those who can live in them I can only wish that they fare forward and fare well. I find my story different and presently necessary, and I also find that I need to claim no more for it than that. That will suffice.[20]

For Crossan, then, "story" refers to rafts of our making, to world-webs which we spin from our own imaginations. He finds this situation, in which he is permanently threatened with destruction exhilarating.[21]

The New Testament scholar Werner Kelber, who is not a specialist in the field of parable-interpretation, accurately summarizes the prevailing consensus regarding parabolic speech as one which "exercises demoralizing pressures on 'the project of making a whole out of one's life.' "[22] Kelber's statement shows how widespread this view of parables has become among scholars today.

On the most obvious level, the idea is that people are "de-moral-ized," in the sense that their moralities are relativized. But there is another implication. It is one thing to believe that this life is the only life, and yet to go on trying to contribute to the coherence of the world in which we live. Even the apostle Paul found this prospect so difficult that he advanced the argument that, "If the dead are not raised, 'Let us eat and drink, for tomorrow we die' " (1 Cor 15:32).[23]

But for those who share the postmodernist conviction that death is God, demoralization in the sense of despair would appear to be the expected outcome. How many people would be prepared to make the effort to construct a whole out of their lives in the full conviction that death is absolute master of all existence? Taylor's ideas would prima facie seem to have a good chance of gaining widespread acceptance among today's postmodernists. But it would appear that he is preaching to the converted, for narcissism has become the prevailing mode of being human in America today.

American Narcissism and Psychic Survivors

CHRISTOPHER LASCH, in *The Minimal Self: Psychic Survival in Trouble Times*,[24] provides extensive evidence for the predominance of the narcissistic mode of selfhood in America today. He includes an account of narcissim as it influences the minimalist aesthetic, and he analyzes the positions of the proponents and opponents of narcissism in contemporary psychoanalytic theory and political debate. My interest lies primarily in Lasch's focus on the minimal self, the self that cannot tell the difference, any more than Narcissus could, between the self and the not-self, the self and the other.[25]

Lasch shows how the contemporary self, uncertain of its own outlines, is lost in a world of flickering images, unable to tell the difference between fantasy and reality.[26] Selfhood is equated with the ability to play a variety of roles and to assume an endless variety of chosen identities.[27] Gone, according to Lasch, is any notion of stability in identity, or any sense of one's life "as a life-history or narrative."[28] One reason people no longer see themselves as subjects of a narrative is that they no longer see themselves as subjects at all, but rather as victims.[29] Threatened with disintegration, and by a sense of inner emptiness, the self chooses minimalism in order to survive "selective apathy, emotional disengagement from others, renunciation of the past and the future, a determination to live one day at a time."[30] Psychic survivors travel light; there is no room for a personal life or a personal history.[31]

Lasch observes in passing that the minimal self is completely different from the conception of human personality that was rooted in Judeo-Christian traditions.[32] Although his study is pervaded by nostalgia for traditional conceptions of human personality, he restricts himself for the most part to cultural analysis.

Taylor, in contrast, embraces minimalism and provides the culture of narcissism with a theological rationale. He calls for the death of the self because he experiences postmodernism as liberation. Like Crossan, he believes that to acknowledge death as God is to be freed from illusion. Their claim is open to dispute. Freud, for one, asserted that, "No greater triumph of wish-fulfillment is conceivable" than to deify death.[33]

In any case, it should come as no surprise that those who share Lasch's nostalgia for stability in identity would advocate a return to traditional Christian patterns of identity.

Whereas Taylor holds up the prodigal son's profligacy as an ideal for postmodern selfhood, George W. Stroup offers the prodigal son as the prototype of one who converted and returned to his father's house.[34] Stroup's solution to the contemporary crisis of Christian identity[35] is to recall the individual to membership in the Christian community. The individual can take for his or her own a ready-made identity by agreeing to reinterpret his or her personal experiences in light of the narratives and symbols provided by the Christian tradition.[36] The basic model for one's life is that of Augustine's story of conversion as outlined in the *Confessions*.[37]

Frank Kermode, the distinguished British literary critic, has observed that "the history of modernism could be written as an account of the conflict between excited catastrophe theorists on the one side and panic-stricken reactionaries on the other."[38] This schema would seem to apply reasonably well to contemporary American theology: Crossan and Taylor, at one extreme, delighting in and excited by the brave new world emerging from the destruction of traditional Christianity; at the other extreme, those who view the postmodern condition with alarm and who would offer solace and direction to the disoriented.

What Has Jesus to Do with Postmodernism?

BOTH PARTIES CLAIM to speak for the Christian tradition. Stroup obviously does so, but even Taylor, who views the entire Christian tradition as an effort to deny death,[39] presents his a/-theology as "radical Christology."[40] Crossan claims to discover his theology not only in the parables of Kafka and Borges, but also in the parables of the historical Jesus. The function of Jesus' parables, like that of all parables, it is claimed, is to "subvert world."[41] The parables:

> are stories which shatter the deep structure of our accepted world and thereby render clear and evident to us the relativity of story itself. They remove our defences and make us vulnerable to God. It is only in such experiences that God can touch us, and only in such moments does the kingdom of God arrive. My own term for this relationship is transcendence.[42]

One should not be misled by the conventional theological vocabulary here. We have already seen that "transcendental experience" is Crossan's term for the thrill one feels as one's world is being destroyed. The advent of the kingdom of God is really for Crossan the arrival of death's dominion.

Now the proposition that the parables of Jesus function to bring about a reversal of human expectations, in order to subvert world, and so exert a demoralizing pressure on the project of fashioning a whole out of one's life, is a claim that can be verified or falsified empirically by examining the authentic sayings and parables of the historical Jesus. It seems to me to be quite legitimate to question whether Jesus shared the assumption that God's power destroys all human constructs, whether Jesus acknowledged death as God, and whether Jesus advocated the minimalist mode of being human. To answer the question adequately is a much more complicated undertaking than would at first appear to be the case. Those of us entrusted with the resources and the responsibility for generating knowledge and understanding of the Christian tradition can and should ask what relationship postmodernist theologies, which present themselves in Christian guise, have with the historical Jesus.

Is death the ultimate reality? This is the most radical question arising from postmodern experience. It cannot be answered in the abstract, through intelletual debate. What historical-critical analysis can achieve is the identification of the ontological and theological assumptions implied in various texts. For example, we can observe that traditional conceptions of human personality have been connected with the belief that the ultimate reality is a transcendent God, whereas minimalist modes of being human emerge in conjunction with the conviction that death is the ultimate reality. The truth about reality cannot be discovered by intellectual analysis, but this does not mean that what we believe to be the case about reality is a matter of indifference, as intellectual nihilists hold.[43] Rather I would affirm that one can discover which mode of being human is grounded in the real only by living out the consequences of what one takes to be ultimate. Moreover, we can be certain that there will indeed be very real consequences.

Which criteria are appropriate for discriminating among the various understandings of what it means to be a Christian? This is a contentious question, and an especially urgent one today. Scheler, for example, in defending Christian love against Nietzsche's charge that it was the most delicate flower of *ressentiment*, never offered a specific set of criteria for distinguishing what "truly Christian love" is, as opposed to the adulterated versions. His arguments, though laced with many valuable distinctions and observations, had the charcter of assertions which may or may not be found persuasive.[44] Insofar as the Christian tradition claims a connection with the historical man Jesus, research concerning the authentic parables and sayings of the historical Jesus should have something to contribute to the debate about what is "Christian."

WHAT COUNTS AS EVIDENCE?

THE FIRST STEP is to determine what materials in the tradition count as evidence. How do we go about this task? One possibility is to begin with some picture of Jesus, one built through historical inference and reconstruction, and then to see how much of the material fits this picture. This has frequently been the practice in historical-Jesus research. Some current opinions are (1) that Jesus was a simple Galilean Jew, a charismatic Hasid, the view of Geza Vermes;[45] (2) that Jesus was the first Christian and the founder of Christianity, the view of C. H. Dodd;[46] (3) that Jesus was an eschatological prophet like John the Baptist, the dominant view in New Testament scholarship today and for most of this century.[47] What underlies these approaches is the idea that only a certain number of historical options were available to Jesus by which to constitute his being, and that the Jesus of history had to choose from the range of options offered by his historical circumstances.[48]

Another method involves suspending judgment from the outset about Jesus, whereby one refuses to start with a picture of him, but attempts to discern whether there might have been something strange and unfamiliar about him. In my opinion, this approach makes the most sense methodologically because it is the easiest hypothesis to test. If this simple, and most radical, hypothesis turned up nothing dissimilar in the Jesus tradition, then it could be abandoned and new hypotheses based on historical inferences developed and tried. When one tests a hypothesis, refutations are final. The hypothesis that there is nothing dissimilar in the Jesus tradition can be rejected now because application of the criterion of dissimilarity turns up at least eight sayings and twelve parables dissimilar from all the sayings and parables extant from Jesus' precursors, contemporaries, and successors.[49]

Some further remarks regarding the use of the criterion of dissimilarity are in order here. In the first place, we do not simply discard the sayings and parables in the Jesus tradition that lie outside the core. In principle, we must be able to write the history of the synoptic tradition, moving outward from the core material and demonstrating in each case the provenance of each and every saying and parable in the tradition. This work is presently being carried out by numerous New Testament scholars.[50] In the second place, it is possible to compare the parables of Jesus with the extant parabolic narratives from late Western antiquity to confirm empirically whether his parables were dissimilar from those of other ancient storytellers. For eight years I directed a research project, funded by the Social Sciences and Humanities Research Council of Canada, whose purpose was to collect all the stories from all the extant literature of late Western antiquity from the death of Alexander to the accession of Constantine (that is, from approximately 323 B.C.E. to the early fourth century C.E., covering both the Hellenistic and the

Greco-Roman periods). From this research I discovered that there are hundreds of stories about fathers with two sons, hundreds of stories about travelers in distress helped or not helped by passers-by, and so on. There are hundreds of parallels to each of the parables of Jesus. However, of several thousand stories collected, using the criteria of narrative theory[51] *not one* of these stories is similar to any of the core parables of Jesus, though there are similarities to early Christian parables. Jesus' parables were dissimilar from all those extant to three hundred years before his time and three hundred years after him. This does not prove, of course, that Jesus was unique; that is a claim that can only be made from the viewpoint of Christian faith.[52] But this research does prove in the scientific sense that Jesus' parables were dissimilar from all extant contemporary stories.

THE TASK OF RECONSTRUCTION

HAVING ISOLATED the core material, that is, the sayings and parables in the Jesus tradition which are dissimilar, the next step is to reconstruct, in so far as our methods allow, the words of the authentic sayings and parables. The tools used in this reconstruction are the familiar ones of source, form, and redaction criticism, supplemented at times by literary criticism.

I would like to observe about this second step that statements about the identity and wording of the sayings and parables of Jesus are descriptive statements. Since they are statements about what is or is not the case, there is the possibility of falsification by other scholars. In other words, statements about what sayings and parables Jesus himself composed are contingent propositions, and are in principle open to confirmation or falsification. This means that everyone who agrees to abide by rational procedures for decision-making should in principle be able to agree that (1) at least these sayings and parables were composed by Jesus, and that (2) these reconstructed sayings and parables contain Jesus' words and not someone else's. My identifications and reconstructions of the sayings and parables of Jesus are provided as an appendix to *The Silence of Jesus*.[53] In what follows, I simply ask the reader to agree to entertain provisionally the hypothesis that the historical Jesus uttered these sayings and parables, so that I can proceed to the more vexing question of their meaning.

After identifying and reconstructing the sayings and parables, the third step is to inquire about their meaning. I am of course aware that the interpretive process carries with it a much lower degree of certainty than do steps one and two. At this, the hermeneutical level, we are inevitably involved in a continuous process of moving back and forth between the core material in its historical-cultural context, on the one hand, and our contemporary situation, on the other. We attempt to make explicit our own hermeneutical presuppositions and expect help from other critically aware participants in the process of identifying any assumptions that have gone unnoticed.

As Hans-Georg Gadamer affirms in *Truth and Method*, we understand only when we understand the question to which something is the answer.[54] If we are to understand the parables of Jesus, we must first understand the question to which the texts are an answer.[55]

The evangelists themselves have offered answers to the question, "What is the question?" Luke, for example, suggests that the story of the man going down the road is an answer to the question, "Who is my neighbor?" Luke believes that the parables of the lost—that is, the lost sheep, the lost coin, and the prodigal son—all provide an answer to the question posed by the Pharisees, "Why does Jesus receive sinners and eat with them?" Matthew suggests that the story of the man who went out early in the morning to hire laborers for his vineyard provides an answer to the disciples' question, "What will we have as our reward, since we have left everything and followed you?" Again, Matthew believes that the story of the man who once gave a dinner and invited guests is the answer to the question about the respective fates of the Jews who rejected Jesus and the Christians who accepted his invitation to the messianic banquet. All of the evangelists' proposed questions can be shown by source, form, and redaction criticism to be secondary, Christian efforts to answer the question, "What is the question?" Thus we cannot use their questions to reconstruct what question Jesus posed or answered.

What, then, does internal analysis of the parables yield? In the case of the sayings of Jesus, it is possible by internal analysis to reconstruct the question. For example, when Jesus said, "The kingdom of God is not coming with signs to be observed; nor will they say, 'Lo, here it is!' or 'There!' for behold the kingdom of God is in the midst of you" (Luke 17:20b-21), it is appropriate to infer that Jesus is speaking in response to a question regarding eschatological signs. Or when Jesus said, "If it is by the finger of God that I cast out demons, then the kingdom of God has come upon you" (Q: Matt 12:18/Luke 11:20), we can, I believe, reasonably infer that Jesus is speaking in response to a question regarding his activity as an exorcist.

THE GAP IN JESUS' STORIES

IN GENERAL TERMS, if a story gives an answer, then we can reconstruct the question. Unlike Jesus' sayings, however, the parables yield from internal analysis no sign as to the question or questions to which they respond. Since Jesus' stories do not give answers, it is doubly difficult to know how to the answer the question, "What is the question?"

Theoretical models of narrative[56] are useful for analysis because they provide a means of asking questions and a sort of template against which to compare the stories composed by different storytellers. Several years ago, in a seminar on the parables, I was working through Daniel Patte's book, *What Is Structural Exegesis?*[57] Patte's theoretical model is a structuralist one derived ultimately from Vladimir Propp's work on Russian fairy tales via the French structuralist Algirdas Greimas. This model predicts that all stores will have a final sequence which is correlated to the initial sequence. According to the theory, the final sequence of any story will correlate with the initial sequence by reestablishing a social order or contract that was disrupted in the initial correlated sequence. Now in Patte's treatment of the story that most people know as "The Good Samaritan," he observes that "This final correlated sequence is not actualized in our text."[58] The structuralist model provides a hypothesis regarding narrative structures which can be verified or falsified empirically. It has real value as a working hypothesis, it seems to me, only if we do not force all stories into a straightjacket but admit that some stories might not fit the model. To say that the final correlated sequence is not *actualized* in Jesus' parable does not go far enough, for the implication is that there is necessarily a final correlated sequence, that is, an *ending* to the story. Attempting to apply the structuralist model led me to conclude that instead of a *final* correlated sequence, the parable closes with another *initial* sequence in which the Samaritan becomes a subject who mandates the innkeeper to carry out the contract of helping the man who was going down the road, was beaten, and was left half-dead by the robbers. In other words, the third man (this is my theological conclusion) communicates his own vitality to the innkeeper. What is important to observe here, and what Patte's structuralist model first led me to recognize, is the idea that Jesus told a story without end.

This prompted me to wonder whether all of Jesus' parables manifested this phenomenon, namely, that Jesus told stories without endings. What would be the meaning of this phenomenon?

Paying close attention to Jesus' parables reveals that we will never know whether the man going down the road ever regained consciousness or whether the third man was ever rewarded for his actions. We will never know whether the man who had two sons was ever reconciled with the elder. We will never know whether the householder who went out early in the morning to hire laborers for his vineyard ever subsequently devised a satisfactory working relationship with them. Nor will we ever know whether the man who once gave a dinner and invited guests ever did find people to entertain. There is a permanent gap where the ending should be in all of the stories Jesus narrated.[59] What does it mean that Jesus told stories without endings?

There are those who claim that not only did Jesus not give answers, but that his parables, to paraphrase Kelber, de-moralize all efforts to make a whole out of one's life. According to Crossan, the parables are vehicles of the force that destroys all human efforts to generate meaning, and so there is nothing to do but play irrelevant games to prepare ourselves for the inevitable end.[60] I do not share this view of how the parables function. Rather, I will argue in these chapters that they function to restore to our consciousness an awareness of a *genuine* ambiguity in the actions of characters. This ambiguity is completely different from postmodernist polyvalence, which claims that parables can mean anything at all, and in fact mean nothing at all. Postmodernist readings, in my view, represent a radical attempt to stamp out ambiguity (and meaning) in order to enforce one, predictable reading—the nihilistic one.[61] On the other hand, it is not my view that parables function in order to provide ready-made plots for those looking for a framework for constructing their identity.

I close this chapter by posing a series of questions. If Jesus is the answer, that is, if the authentic sayings and parables of the historical Jesus are to be the criterion for our theological reflection, the question is, "What is the question?" Jesus' parables themselves do not provide an answer to this question. We must then proceed to pose our own questions, which we bring to the parables from our postmodernist situations. These questions include: Is death God? Does living in story arise (as the postmodernists claim) solely from the effort to deny death? What does it mean to exist as a person? Is living in story a distinctive mode of being human? Is it rooted in a perception regarding what power is ultimate in human experience? Our attempt to pursue these questions will resume in the next chapter, where I consider the topic of "Narrative Decisions and Moral Choices." I ask whether those who make difficult moral choices in the hope of fashioning a whole out of their lives should be de-moralized by Jesus' parables, as they are by the writing of postmodernist New Testament scholars and theologians.

2

Narrative Decisions and Moral Choices

IN THE FIRST ESSAY, I asked: If Jesus is the answer, what is the question? That is, if we agree that understanding the authentic sayings and parables of the historical Jesus can help us identify the marks that characterize the Christian tradition, then we need to determine what the question addressed by Jesus' saying and parables was. Focusing on the core phonodramatic parables led to the observation that they do not function to give answers: They tell stories with permanent gaps—without endings. In other words, the question is: What is the question? In the world of the parables, we never know who wins and who loses, who succeeds and who fails, who is rewarded and who is punished. What is the meaning of this phenomenon? Does it mean that Jesus' parables are amoral or even antimoral? Are people who make difficult moral choices in the hope of fashioning a whole out of their lives to be de-moralized by the parables, as they are by the words of postmodernist New Testament scholars and theologians?

Life Grounded in the Real

THE SENSE THAT our decisions do make a difference is perhaps best communicated in Robert Frost's "The Road Not Taken":

Two roads diverged in a yellow wood
and sorry I could not travel both
And be one traveler, long I stood
And looked down one as far as I could;
To where it bent in the undergrowth;

Then took the other, as just as fair,
And perhaps having the better claim,
Because it was grassy and wanted wear;
Though as for that the passing there
Had worn them really about the same,
And both that morning equally lay
In leaves no step had trodden black.
Oh, I kept the first for another day!
Yet knowing how way leads on to way,
I doubted if I should ever come back.

I shall be telling this with a sigh
Somewhere ages and ages hence:
Two roads diverged in a wood, and I—
I took the one less traveled by,
And that has made all the difference.[1]

The narrator could not travel both roads and be one traveler. This is the feature of Frost's poem that claims my attention. Given the way the narrator posits his human being, his choices are mutually exclusive. In fact, he could have gone a little way on one road, and then after a while backtracked to the fork in the road to sample the other way. But he could not travel both roads and be one traveler. The stability of his identity is somehow tied to making a choice that entails further choices, all of them mutually exclusive. Making such choices to maintain the integrity of one's identity is one possible view of what it means to live in story.

This sense of the intimate relationship between being one traveler and not attempting to travel more than one road, is one which, according to Christopher Lasch, has been lost in the contemporary world. Lasch explains what we all know, that today the minimalist self reduces choice to a matter of style and taste and believes that no choice can be demonstrated to be inherently preferable to any other choice.[2] Indeed, one need not really make choices: "A society of consumers defines choice not as the freedom to choose one course of action over another but as the freedom to choose everything at once. 'Freedom of choice' means 'keeping your options open.' "[3] Lasch mocks this view and claims that "in *real life* . . . every moral and cultural choice of any consequence rules out a whole series of other choices."[4] Although Lasch does not make the connection explicitly between narrative decisions and moral choices, I would like to emphasize that "seeing one's life as a life history or a narrative" involves repeatedly choosing between two diverging roads. To make a moral choice is to rule out the whole series of possibilities beckoning along the road not taken. Indeed, organizing one's being morally is incompatible with acting in order to keep one's options open. Lasch asserts that choosing alternatives which rule out others is real life; he labels choices aimed at keeping one's options open "pluralist fantasy."

The question I would like to ask is whether Lasch is correct in his assertion regarding "real life." The answer depends on what one means by "real life." If one means the everyday world, then Lasch is clearly wrong, for his whole book serves to collect evidence about the narcissistic modes of being human, which show no interest in being one traveler. Minimal selves prefer to choose everything and to keep their options open. On the other hand, if by "real life" Christopher Lasch means not "everyday life as we know it," but "life that is grounded in reality," then we have an issue worthy of pursuit. Does life grounded in the real involve moral choices that rule out a whole series of other choices? This depends on one's notion of anthropology and ontology; or, in our terms, what it means to be a person and what it means to live in story.

The Sense of an Ending

THE ISSUES CAN BE set in the wide context of the contemporary debate concerning what narrative theorists term "closure." To introduce what is at stake in the debate about "closure" and to communicate a sense of what "closure" does in stories, I quote the Christian theologian A. E. Harvey:

> A story needs an ending. A point must be reached at which one can feel that certain issues are resolved, a certain finality has been achieved. In this respect a story departs from real life. In reality there never is an end. Life goes on, and what seemed like a critical or decisive moment at the time turns out to be just another phase of the endlessly varied pattern of human existence. Even death—which is most eagerly seized on by novelists as a genuine punctuation mark in the long and complicated sentences of life—turns out in our experience to be no end at all. New events spring from it immediately, there is no pause in the continual drama of life. But the storyteller cannot accept this. He cannot make his story meaningful unless, by giving it an end, he can show who wins and loses, who is rewarded and who punished, who succeeds and who fails. The never-ending progress of real life

leaves every question open; new events may alter the judgment passed on the old, unforeseen consequences may cause previous decisions to be seen in a new light. The story-teller needs finality, a closed sequence of events such that a judgment can be passed. He needs to impose something which does not exist in the real world: an ending. . . . What I am describing is of course more than a literary convention. It is an essential device for making sense of our experience. Unless we postulate an end towards which our efforts are tending, or which will relieve us from our suffering, our life becomes meaningless and unendurable.[5]

CLOSURE AS USEFUL FICTION

CLOSURE THEN IS the sense of an ending,[6] the sense that a series of events can be judged to be meaningful because of the outcome of that series. According to Harvey, in real life there never is a point at which the meaning of our experience becomes clear. Indeed, our lives would be meaningless and unendurable if we could not impose on our experience something which, according to Harvey, does not exist in the real world: the sense of an ending.[7] Human beings require a sequence of events in a story to give a kind of finality that enables us to judge who wins and who loses, who is rewarded and who punished, who succeeds and who fails. Closed endings to stories, in this view, are an essential device for making sense of our experience. According to Harvey, closure is a useful fiction.

Frank Kermode makes a point similar to Harvey's in an essay entitled "Secrets and Narrative Sequence."[8] He begins the essay quoting an amusing piece of verse:

Lucinda can't read poetry. She's good,
Sort of, at novels, though. The words, you know,
Don't sort of get in like Lucinda's way.

> And then the story, well, you know, about
> Real people, fall in love, like that, and all.
> Sort of makes you think, Lucinda thinks.[9]

As Kermode points out, what enables Lucinda to follow a novel is the story, which is constructed with characters who seem like real people because their actions form a plot. "Plot" is the term for a sequence of events finalized by closure. Lucinda can follow this kind of plot and understand its message. This sort of makes you think, Lucinda thinks. People like Lucinda need closure in stories, the sense that there is a message to be derived from the actions of characters.[10] Lucinda has, no doubt, never wondered whether there are plots in real life.

CLOSURE AS HARMFUL ILLUSION

IT IS AGAINST the Lucindas of the world that the deconstructionists have mounted their attack. They, unlike Harvey, pour scorn on Lucinda's need for endings, precisely because they agree with Harvey that in real life there are no endings that permit us to construe the meaning of events. Termination, the terminal ending caused by death, is the only real ending for the deconstructionists. Their position is that closure is fiction, a harmful, useless, fiction.

Jacques Derrida offers an example of the literary method of deconstruction that states the postmodernist case quite clearly in "The Law of Genre."[11] Derrida argues that we constitute ourselves in narratives as subjects solely because we feel we must, and indeed, desire, to give an account of ourselves to others and to ourselves.[12] People who cannot give an account of themselves are deemed unfit to participate in the prevailing social structures of Western culture, which are rooted in the law, that is, the impulse to judge and to control. According to Derrida, the law that elicits and uses such life-stories (or genres) is in effect madness. In other words, there are no plots in "real" life, only in madness; and genre is "madness."[13] The law demands that we give a narrative account of ourselves. Those willing to constitute themselves as subjects of narratives and to give an account of themselves to others respond obligingly to this demand. From this perspective, life-stories are fundamentally a means of psycho-sociological control of ourselves and others.

In "The Value of Narrativity in the Representation of Reality," the historian Hayden White also claims that real events do not offer themselves as plots.[14] White claims that the impulse to narrativize events is rooted purely in a psychological need. He asks, "What wish is enacted, what desire is gratified by the fantasy that real events are properly represented when they can be shown to display the formal coherency of a story?"[15] He answers that every fully realized story "is a kind of allegory, points to a moral, or endows events, whether real or imaginary, with a significance that they do not possess as mere sequence. . . . It seems possible to conclude that every historical narrative has as its latent or manifest purpose the desire to moralize the events of which it treats."[16] According to White, the impulse to moralize is a strategy "for making the real desirable, making the real into an object of desire, and does so by its imposition, upon events, that are represented as real, of the formal coherency that stories possess."[17] The reason that the real is made desirable, according to White, is that, in (moralizing) narrative, "reality wears the mask of meaning, the completeness and fullness of which we can only imagine, but never experience. That is, historical narrative displays to us a formal coherency that we ourselves lack."[18] The core of his argument is that "the notion that sequences of real events possess the formal attributes of the stories we tell about imaginary events could only have its origin in wishes, daydreams, reveries."[19] He ends his essay by asking the question (to which he expects a negative answer): "Could we ever narrativize without moralizing?"[20]

If we consider for a moment the human need for closure from the point of view of the postmodernists, it is not difficult to appreciate their objections. We have seen how A. E. Harvey, for example, speaks approvingly of the human need to know who wins and who loses, who is rewarded and who punished, who succeeds and who fails. He appears to view closure as a fiction useful for lending human life a coherence and meaning it does not inherently possess. Crossan's view is similar.[21] If living in story is no more than a device for making sense out of our experience, then perhaps White is correct in implying that those who live in story are living in fantasy, not reality. The anthropological question and the ontological question are inextricably related here.

CLOSURE AS SELF-ACCOUNTING

THE POSITION AGAINST which the deconstructionists, including the postmodernist a/theologian Mark C. Taylor, inveigh can again be best represented by George W. Stroup. For Stroup, the classic form of Christian narrative by which Christians are to constitute their identity is Augustine's *Confessions*. Stroup claims that "it is universally and primordially the case that the articulation of personal identity assumes the form of a narrative."[22] What kind of narratives does Stroup have in mind? "In order to identify ourselves to another person or persons, in order to explain what kind of person we are and why we are the way we are, we recite a narrative that recounts and interprets personal history."[23] Notice that Stroup's language indicates his implicit assumption that we tell stories to give an account of ourselves to an "other."[24] He has in mind other Christians in the Christian community and, of course, the big "Other," God. For Stroup, a Christian's story is a "confession" based on the classic model laid out by Augustine.[25] This narrative interprets human existence "by means of the paired realities of grace and sin. If the Christian claim is that faith is a human response to God's grace and that this response entails transformation and redemption, then these theological categories should have visible consequences in the stories Christians tell about themselves."[26]

Is it universally and primordially the case that the articulation of human identity assumes the shape of a formally coherent narrative? This to me is clearly not so, as Christopher Lasch's accumulation of evidence regarding the minimal self shows. Those who understand themselves as psychic survivors, as consumers, as victims struggling merely to survive, or as vagrants or bums, do not live in the kinds of narrative Stroup has in mind. Nor do the postmodernists. Taylor adopts a new "identity" as an anonymous trace, as a weaver of other people's ideas. Certainly Jesus did not assume that one of the conditions for being human was possession of a capacity for living in story. The rich man's steward, for example, construes his predicament as that of one to whom things happen, as a victim. He says, "What shall I do, since my master is taking the stewardship away from me?" He understands himself not in terms of a history but in terms of his qualities—as weak and vain. He says, "I am not strong enough to dig, and I am ashamed to beg."[27] It seems clear to me that not everyone lives in story, not everyone makes the moral choices necessary for sustaining a stable identity.

The issue here is whether the impulse to make narrative decisions in one's existence is inextricably connected with the dictates of morality and law, which demand that we give an account of ourselves. Is the impulse to narrativize human existence always bound up with the urge to judge ourselves and others? Do people who posit their being in story do so solely in order that they may participate in the prevailing mechanisms for psychological and sociological control, as Derrida argues?[28]

Paul Ricoeur has outlined a case for the pro-closure party.[29] He makes an effort to ground ontologically both the human experience of temporality and the notion of "plot," that is, stories with closure. After arguing that temporality is constitutive of human consciousness,[30] Ricoeur goes on to assert that plots are in fact found in real life.[31] He claims that human beings are entangled in plots[32] and that to narrate them is simply to make known the plot.[33] Ricoeur argues that there are plots in "real life" and that storytellers simply narrate the "untold stories of our lives."[34]

Stories with closure allow us to evaluate the actions of the characters and to draw inferences concerning what actions are valid or invalid. Ricoeur claims that there is no action that does not give rise to "approbation" or "reprobation," that an action can never be ethically neutral.[35] Narrative, in his view, responds to a universal human impulse to pass judgment on the actions of others and of themselves, and Ricoeur would argue that this need corresponds to the way reality is ordered. Put simply, for Ricoeur there are plots in real life. In his view, human lives inherently possess moral meaning. The deconstructionists, the anti-closure party, would vehemently deny this. In the middle are theologians like Harvey who believe that closure is a useful fiction.

Ricoeur bases his case regarding temporality on an analysis of Augustine's *Confessions*[36] and his case for plot on a reading of Aristotle's *Poetics*.[37] This case is hardly likely to convince the deconstructionists, however comforting it might be to those who favour Paul Ricoeur's view. Augustine, after all, represents the culmination of centuries of the Christian mode of being human, one grounded in a specific set of anthropological, ontological, and theological assumptions. Furthermore, Aristotle, given his preference for periodic structures, especially for stories with plots or moral meanings, can hardly be called a neutral witness in the debate about closure.[38]

Closure in Ancient Storytelling

THE VIEW THAT to be human entails the making of moral choices is not distinctively Christian. Centuries prior to the appearance of Jesus, the Greeks, fascinated by the problem of moral choice, had considered this mode of being human.[39] In Xenophon's *Memorabilia* (2.1.32-34), Hercules must:

> choose between two ways of life represented for him by two women. The one, Virtue, was tall, erect, and dressed in white; the other, Vice, looked taller than she was, tended to fleshiness, used make-up in order to look more rosy and wore a semi-transparent dress. The former ate only when hungry, the latter whenever she wanted; Vice also looked for snow to keep herself cool in summer and when she went to bed put on heavy rugs to keep herself warm.[40]

This notion of choice pervades Greek thought and culture. In the earlier period of Greek thinking, evidenced in their mythology, it was the gods who rewarded the virtuous and punished the wicked.[41] By the fifth century, before Aristotle's time, this system had evolved into the idea that failure was due to moral defect and success due to moral virtue,[42] an idea that continued to be developed for centuries in the philosophical schools.[43]

Just how deeply ingrained this moralizing view of the world was in the apperceptions of the ancients can be illustrated by considering some selections from among the stories I have collected from late Western antiquity.[44] Every single extant story, Greek, Roman, or Jewish, exhibits closure, or if closure is lacking in the events of the story, the narrator intervenes to award approbation or reprobation to the characters.[45] I will give some examples, selecting only from parallels to Jesus' story of the man going down the road.

MYTHS

IN THE FIRST GROUP, the gods themselves reward those who give help to travelers in distress and punish those who do not:

Closure occurs within the course of events. The first example is from Ovid's *Metamorphoses*:

No, young man, no mountain-deity dwells in this altar. She claims its worship, whom the queen of heaven once shut out from all the world, whom wandering Delos would scarce accept at her prayer, when it was an island, lightly floating on the sea. There reclining on the palm and Pallas' tree, in spite of their step-mother, she brought forth her twin babes. Even thence the new-made mother is said to have fled from Juno, carrying in her bosom her infant children both divine. And now, having reached the borders of Lycia, home of the Chimaera, when the hot sun beat fiercely upon the fields, the goddess, weary of her long struggle, was faint by reason of the sun's heat and parched with thirst; and the hungry children had drained her breasts dry of milk. She chanced to see a lake of no great size down in a deep vale; some rustics were there gathering bushy osiers, with fine swamp-grass and rushes of the marsh. Latona came to the water's edge and kneeled on the ground to quench her thirst with a cooling draught. But the rustic rabble would not let her drink.

Then she besought them: "Why do you deny me water? The enjoyment of water is a common right. Nature has not made the sun private to any, nor the air, nor soft water. This common right I seek; and yet I beg you to give it to me as a favour. I was not preparing to bathe my limbs or my weary body here in your pool, but only to quench my thirst. Even as I speak, my mouth is dry of moisture, my throat is parched, and my voice can scarce find utterance. A drink of water will be nectar to me, and I shall confess that I have received life with it; yes, life you will be giving me if you let me drink. These children too, let them touch your hearts, who from my bosom stretch out their little arms."

And it chanced that the children did stretch out their arms. Who would not have been touched by the goddess' gentle words? Yet for all her prayers they persisted in de-

nying with threats if she did not go away; they even added
insulting words. Not content with that, they soiled the
pool itself with their feet and hands, and stirred up the
soft mud from the bottom, leaping about, all for pure
meanness.

Then wrath postponed thirst; for Coeus' daughter
could neither humble herself longer to those unruly fel-
lows, nor could she endure to speak with less power than
a goddess; but stretching up her hands to heaven, she
cried: "Live then for ever in that pool." It fell out as the
goddess prayed.

It is their delight to live in water; now to swim upon the
surface. Often they sit upon the sedgy bank and often
leap back into the cool lake. But even now, as of old, they
exercise their foul tongues in quarrel, and all shameless,
though they may be under water, even under the water
they try to utter maledictions. Now also their voices are
hoarse, their inflated throats swell up, and their constant
quarrelling distends their wide jaws; they stretch their
ugly heads, the necks seem to have disappeared. Their
backs are green; their bellies, the largest part of the body,
are white; as new-made frogs they leap in the muddy
pool.[46]

The peasants have refused to help a goddess in disguise, and
have been punished for their lack of hospitality, providing an example of how justice is guaranteed in the course of events by
the gods.

In another story from the *Metamorphoses*, the story of Lycaon, Book 1, Jupiter tells how he went down to earth to find
out whether men were impious or not:

I had crossed Menala bristling with the lairs of beasts, Cy-
lene and the pine groves of chill Lycaon. Thence I ap-
proached the seat and inhospitable abode of the Arcadian
king, just as the late evening shades were ushering in the
night. I gave a sign that a god had come, and the common

folk had begun to worship me. Lycaon at first mocked at
their pious prayers, and then he said: "I will soon find out,
and that by a plain test, whether this fellow be god or
mortal, nor shall the truth be at all in doubt." He planned
that night while I was heavy with sleep to kill me by an
unexpected, murderous attack. Such was the experiment
which he adopted to test the truth.

As it turns out, Jupiter punished him "with his avenging bolt, he
o'erthrew the house upon its master and its guilty household."[47]

Another example is the story of Philemon and Baucis, a humble couple who, without knowing it, give hospitality to the gods
and are rewarded with a temple in which to serve as priest and
priestess to the gods. Then when they die, they are changed
into ivy and a tree, which will grow together forever.[48]

The idea of providing hospitality to travelers was deeply ingrained in the ancient world and, in some of the stories and
myths, we find the notion that there would be a divine reward
or a divine punishment, depending on whether one helped
travelers in need of assistance.[49]

I now cite a rabbinic example of this type of story:

> Abba Tahnah the pious was entering his city on the Sab-
> bath-eve at dusk with his bundle slung over his shoulder,
> when he met a man afflicted with boils lying at the cross-
> road. The latter said to him, "Rabbi, do me an act of char-
> ity and carry me into the city." He remarked, "If I aban-
> don my bundle, from where shall I and my household
> support ourselves? But if I abandon this afflicted man I
> will forfeit my life!"
>
> What did he do? He allowed the Good Inclination to
> master the Evil Inclination and carried the afflicted man
> into the city. He then returned for his bundle and entered
> at sunset. Everybody was astonished and exclaimed, "Is
> this Abba Tahnah the pious?" He too felt uneasy in his
> heart and said, "Do you think that I perhaps desecrated
> the Sabbath?"

At that time the Holy One, blessed be He, caused the sun to shine, as it is written, "But unto you that fear My name shall the sun of righteousness arise" (Mal 3:7,20). He again felt uneasy and said, "Do you think that my reward has not been received?" A *Bath Kol* went forth and said to him, "Go thy way, eat thy bread with God, and drink thy wine with a merry heart, for God hath already accepted thy works, thy reward has been received."[50]

LEGENDS AND ANECDOTES

In a second group of stories, the virtuous are rewarded for their actions in the natural course of events. A Jewish example is a story told about Rabbi Eleazar. The implication is that the Torah orders reality in such a way that the virtuous will succeed mightily:

R. Eleazar b. Shammua was walking on the rocks by the sea, when he saw a ship which was tossed about in the water suddenly sink with all on board. He noticed a man sitting on a plank of the ship [carried] from wave to wave until he stepped ashore. Being naked he hid himself among the rocks by the sea.

It happened to be the time for the Israelite to go up to Jerusalem for the Festival. He said to them, "I belong to the descendants of Esau, your brother; give me a little clothing wherewith to cover my nakedness because the sea stripped me bare and nothing was saved with me." They retorted, "So may all your people be stripped bare!" He raised his eyes and saw R. Eleazar who was walking among them, he exclaimed, "I observe that you are an old and respected man of your people, and you know the respect due to your fellow-creatures. So help me, and give me a garment wherewith to cover my nakedness because the sea stripped me bare." R. Eleazar b. Shammua was wearing seven robes; he took one off and gave it to him.

He also led him to his house, provided him with food and
drink, gave him two hundred *dinars*, drove him fourteen
Persian miles, and treated him with great honour until he
brought him to his own home. Some time later the wicked
emperor died, and they elected this man king in his stead,
and he decreed concerning that province that all the men
were to be killed and all the women taken as spoil. They
said to R. Eleazar b. Shammua, "Go and intercede for us."
He told them, "You know that this government does nothing without being paid." They said to him, "Here are four
thousand *dinars*; take them and go and intercede for us."
He took them and went and stood by the gate of the royal
palace. He said to [the guards], "Go, tell the king that a
Jew is standing at the gate, and wishes to greet the king."
The king ordered him to be brought in. On beholding him
the king descended from his throne and prostrated himself before him. He asked him, "What is my master's business here, and why has my master troubled to come
here?" He replied, "That you should have mercy upon
this province and annul this decree." The king asked him,
"Is there any falsehood written in the Torah?" "No," was
the reply; and he said to him, "Is it not written in your Torah, *An Ammonite or a Moabite shall not enter into the as-
sembly of the Lord* (Deut 23:4)?' What is the reason? 'Because they met you not with bread and with water in the
way (Deut 23:5). It is also written, 'Thou shalt not abhor
an Edomite, for he is thy brother (Deut 23:8); and am I
not a descendant of Esau, your brother, but they did not
treat me with kindness! And whoever transgresses the Torah incurs the penalty of death." R. Eleazar b. Shammua
replied to him, "Although they are guilty towards you,
forgive them, and have mercy upon them." He said to
him, "You know that this government does nothing without being paid." He told him, "I have with me four thousand *dinars*; take them and have mercy upon the people."
He said to him, "These four thousand *dinars* are presented to you in exchange for the two hundred which you
gave me, and the whole province will be spared for your

sake in return for the food and drink with which you provided me. Go also into my treasury and take seventy robes
of honour in return for the robe you gave me, and go in
peace to your people whom I forgive for your sake." They
applied to him the text, "Cast thy bread upon the
waters."[51]

Yet stories dealing with events that have actually happened
will not always have suitable endings. Clearly the deconstructionists have a point. A story by Seneca shows how in real life
one might have to wait a while for events to turn out as one
would like:

Philip, king of the Macedonians, had a soldier who was
a valiant fighter, and, having found his services useful in
many campaigns, he had from time to time presented him
with some of the booty as a reward for his prowess, and,
by his repeated bounties, was exciting the venal spirit of
the man. Once after being shipwrecked he was cast
ashore upon the estate of a certain Macedonian; this one,
when he heard the news, rushed to his help, resuscitated
his breath, brought him to his farmhouse, surrendered to
him his bed, restored him from a weak and half-dead condition to new life, cared for him for thirty days at his own
expense, put him upon his feet, provided him with money
for his journey, and heard him say over and over: "I will
show you my gratitude if only I have the good fortune to
see my commander." To Philip he gave an account of his
shipwreck, but said nothing of the help he had received,
and promptly asked Philip to present him with a certain
man's estate. The man was, in fact, his host, the very one
who had rescued him, who had restored him to health.
Kings sometimes, especially in time of war, make many
gifts with their eyes closed. "One just man is no match for
so many armed men fired with greed, it is not possible for
any mortal to be a good man and a good general at the
same time. How will he satiate so many thousands of in-

satiable men? What will they have if every man has only what is his own?" So Philip communed with himself as he gave orders that the soldier should be put in possession of the property he asked for. The other, however, when he was expelled from his property, did not, like a peasant, endure his wrong in silence, thankful that he himself had not been included in the presents, but wrote a concise and outspoken letter to Philip. Upon receiving this, Philip was so enraged that he immediately ordered Pausanias to restore the property to its former owner, and, besides, to brand that most dishonourable of soldiers, most ungrateful of guests, most greedy of shipwrecked men with letters showing him to be an ungrateful person. He, indeed, deserved, not merely to be branded with those letters, but to have them carved in his flesh—a man who had cast out his own host to lie like a naked and shipwrecked sailor upon that shore on which he himself had lain. But we shall heed within what limits the punishment ought to be kept; he had, in any case, to be deprived of what he had seized with the utmost villainy. Yet who would be moved by his punishment? He had committed a crime which could stir no pitiful heart to pity him.[52]

Another group of stories deals with people who were reported actually to have helped others. In these stories, also, the actual course of events does not always provide suitable rewards and punishments. In cases where events provide no plots, the storyteller intervenes in exactly the way Seneca does. The narrator praises those who have done virtuous deeds and blames those who have not acted virtuously; that functions as a substitute for closure:

> Listen then, Toxaris, to the tale of another, Euthydicus of Chalcis. It was repeated to me by Simylus, the sea-captain of Megara, who took his solemn oath that he himself had seen the deed. He said that he was making voyage from Italy to Athens at about the season of the setting of

the Pleiades, carrying a miscellaneous collection of passengers, among whom was Euthydicus, who was vigorous and strong, while Damon was pale and sickly, just convalescing, it seemed, from a prolonged illness.

As far as Sicily they had made a fortunate passage, said Simylus; but when they had run through the straits and in due time were sailing in the Adriatic itself, a great tempest fell upon them. Why repeat the many details of his story—huge seas, cyclones, hail, and all the other evils of a storm? But when they were at last abreast of Zacynthos, sailing with the yard bare, and also dragging hawsers in their wake to check the fury of their driving, towards midnight Damon became seasick, as was natural in weather so rough, and began to vomit, leaning out-board. Then, I suppose because the ship was hove down with greater force towards the side over which he was leaning and the high sea contributed a send, he fell overboard head-first; and the poor fellow was not even without his clothes, so as to have been able to swim more easily. So he began at once to call for help, choking and barely able to keep himself above the water.

When Euthydicus, who happened to be undressed and in his bunk, heard him, he flung himself into the sea, got to Damon, who was already giving out (all this was visible at a long distance because the moon was shining) and helped him by swimming beside him and bearing him up. The rest of them, he said, wanted to aid the men and deplored their misfortune, but could not do it because the wind that drove them was too strong; however, they did at least something, for they threw them a number of pieces of cork and some spars, on which they might swim if they chanced upon any of them, and finally even the gang plank, which was not small.

Think now, in the name of the gods! what firmer proof of affection could a man display towards a friend who had fallen overboard at night into a sea so wild than that of sharing his death? I beg you, envisage the tumult of the seas, the roar of the breaking water, the boiling spume, the night, the despair; then one man struggling, barely keeping up his head, holding his arms out to his friend, and the other leaping after him at once, swimming with him, fearing that Damon would perish first. In that way you can appreciate that in the case of Euthydicus too it is no common friend whom I have described.

TOXARIS: Did the men lose their lives, Minesippus, or were they unaccountably saved, somehow? I am very concerned about them.

MINESIPPUS: Never fear, Toxaris; they were saved and are now at Athens, both of them, studying philosophy. Simylus, to be sure, could only tell this tale about what he had once seen in the night—the one falling overboard, the other leaping after him, and both swimming as long as he could distinguish them in the darkness. But the sequel was told by Euthydicus himself. In the beginning they came upon some corks on which they supported themselves and kept afloat uncomfortably, but afterwards, seeing the gang plank at last, towards daybreak, they swam to it and then, after climbing upon it, easily drifted to Zacynthos.[53]

Another example of the same type occurs in Lucian:

But let me tell you about another man equally honoured, Belitta, cousin of that same Amizoces. He saw that this friend Basthes, had been dragged off his horse by a lion (it chanced that they were hunting together), and already the lion, lying upon him, had fastened upon his throat and was tearing him with his claws. Springing to the ground, he attacked the animal from behind and tried to draw him away, provoking him, diverting his attention, inserting his fingers between his teeth, and endeavoring in every possible way to extract Basthes from the grip of his jaws, until at last the lion left Basthes half-dead and turning upon Belitta, seized and killed him. In dying, however, he at least succeeded in stabbing the lion in the breast with his sword, so that they all died together, and in burying them we made two barrows in close proximity, one for the friends and one facing it for the lion.[54]

FABLES

THE FINAL GROUP of stories I will deal with are the fables, usually, though not always, attributed to Aesop. Here we do not always find the "good" being rewarded and the "bad" being punished. Rather, the clever types succeed and the foolish suffer. Although the ideology differs from the mythological and historical stories, the fables still exhibit closure, leaving no doubt that the behavior we should emulate is that of the clever, while shunning the example of the foolish. Take, for instance, "The Panther and the Shepherds":

> Those who are scorned usually pay in the same coin.
> Once an imprudent panther inadvertently fell into a pit. The country people saw her there. Some of them brought clubs, others piled stones on her; still others *felt sorry* for her, as being likely to die, though no one harmed her, and these tossed bread to her that she might keep herself alive. Night came on and the men went home unconcerned, thinking that they would find her dead on the following day. But the panther, having recruited her failing strength, with a quick leap freed herself from the pit and hastened to her lair at a swift pace. After a few days she sallied forth again, slaughtered the sheep, killed the shepherds themselves, and laid everything waste in the exercise of her violent and savage fury. Hereupon even those who had spared the beast began to be afraid for themselves; they made no complaint about lost property but only begged for their lives. But she said to them: "I remember who attacked me with stones, and who gave me bread. As for you, cease to be afraid; I return as an enemy only to those who injured me."[55]

This fable is a good example of the virtuous at least escaping punishment. Here we see the motif of a distinction between those who pass by and those who give help, those who are compassionate and those who are not, those who are rewarded, those who are punished. The next example is a little different. Here Aesop, quoted by Aristotle in the *Rhetoric*, defends a demagogue who was being tried for his life by relating the following fable:

> A fox, while crossing a river, was driven into a ravine. Being unable to get out, she was for a long time in sore distress, and a number of dog-fleas clung to her skin. A hedgehog, wandering about, saw her and moved with compassion, asked her if he should remove the fleas. The fox refused and when the hedgehog asked the reason, she answered: "They are already full of me and draw little blood; but if you take them away, others will come that are hungry and will drain what remains to me."[56]

I cite this fable for two reasons. First, those who have read *The Silence of Jesus* will see why I do not think it a great loss to Christian theology that we must edit Luke's version of the parable in which a Samaritan showed compassion toward the man he has helped. It is simply not a distinctively Christian idea. In Aesop we have a compassionate hedgehog. I do not believe that Christian love stands or falls on the Samaritan's showing compassion to the beaten man, lying alongside the road. Aesop's fable is doubly interesting because help is refused.

A third kind of story the ancients tell in the fables shows a slightly different idea about helping—sometimes people who help others in distress are thought to be simply foolish. There is a fable about a fox who falls into a well and could not get out. A thirsty goat comes to the well and is tricked by the fox into climbing down into the well. There he was again tricked into allowing the fox to climb over him and out of the well with the promise that the fox will then pull him out. Once free, however, the fox refuses to help the goat.[57] The moral of the story is that sensible people should first discern the ends of an enterprise, before they undertake it. There are numerous fables of people who, by helping others, in fact incur some sort of disadvantage to themselves.[58]

Can One Narrativize without Moralizing?

THE EXAMPLES I have cited should be sufficient to illustrate the point I want to make regarding how dissimilar Jesus' story about the man going down the road is from all of the stories surviving from late Western antiquity that deal with the theme of helping. The third man (or the Samaritan) is not rewarded in the story, nor are the robbers or those who pass by punished. There is not even the minimal closure that would occur if the story told whether or not the man recovered at the inn. A medieval version of "The Good Samaritan" from the *Gospel of Barnabas* fills the gap in Jesus' parable. *Barnabas* adds a scene at the end of the story in which the Samaritan is pictured chatting with the man (who must have regained consciousness), saying to him: "Be of good cheer, for I will speedily return and conduct thee to my own home."[59] Obviously they are then going to establish a personal relationship. And finally, in contrast, Jesus as narrator does not intervene in the parable to comment on the behavior of his characters, by way of approbation or reprobation. Compared with all other ancient stories, Jesus' parable does not exhibit closure, nor does it focalize approval or disapproval.

Let us now return to White's question: Could one ever narrativize without moralizing? Judging from the evidence of all the stories extant from late Western antiquity, the answer would have to be no. That is, there would seem to be support for Ricoeur's affirmation that there is no action that does not give rise to approbation or reprobation, and for Stroup's claim that the impulse to narrativize morally is universal and primordial. All of the stories from late Western antiquity exhibit closure, or, if they do not, either the narrators intervene to judge the actions of their characters or they focalize a set of norms which provide criteria for judging their actions. Stories with closure are by far the dominant type not only in late Western antiquity but also in the whole Western tradition.

Contemporary debate about closure can be divided essentially into two parties: those who champion closure because they believe they can find plots in real life, and those who abhor it because they believe moralizing systems to be the expression of fantasies, daydreams, and desires. For the pro-closure party, the validity of our moralizing stories is guaranteed either by purportedly universal structures of human consciousness and reality, or as a last resort, by an extratextual, extraterrestrial Judge. For the anticlosure party, which includes many New Testament scholars and theologians, death is ultimate, destruction governs all human life, and so all human projects are meaningless, especially the attempt to fashion one's life into the shape of a plotted story. Why not, as Taylor says, live as a vagrant, a pervert, or a bum?

The position of the pro-closure party implies that we cannot know what events mean until they have ended; there must be an ending, in this view, for the coherence of events to be grasped and judged. Or, to put it ontologically, the implication even for the pro-closure party is that death holds the key to the meaning of life. This is not a specifically Christian view. It has been carried over into Christian thinking from the Greeks, who had a maxim that appears in the end of the final chorus of the received editions of Sophocles' *Oedipus Rex*. This saying also appears in Aeschylus's *Agamemnon* (l.928) and elsewhere: "Count no man happy until he's dead."[60] I take this to mean that we have to see the end before we can judge the value of a life. In some Christian traditions the end of life has been understood to be the Last Judgment, at which time we will discover the meaning of our actions: The good will be rewarded and the evil punished.

Do Jesus' parables imply that death holds the key to the meaning of life? The parables, I am afraid, do not come in on the side of the pro-closure party. As I have said, we will never know whether the man going down the road ever regained consciousness or whether the third man was ever rewarded for his actions, whether the man who had two sons was ever reconciled with his elder son, whether the householder who went out early in the morning to hire laborers for his vineyard ever devised a satisfactory working relationship with his hired laborers, or whether the man who once gave a dinner and invited guests ever did find people to entertain for dinner. At the level of story, there is a permanent gap at the end of Jesus' parables.

Furthermore, the narrator never intervenes ideologically to express approbation or reprobation of the actions of any of his characters. In short, and I think this is extremely important: Jesus narrativized without moralizing.

Prompted by the parables of Jesus, I would pose the following question: Can the value of a mode of being human be discerned apart from the consequences, outcomes, or conclusion of that mode of being human? Is there a mode of being human that can be grasped as inherently meaningful, and coherent, as grounded in the real in and of itself, without being evaluated in terms of some external norms?

In the context of this question, I am reminded of Thomas Beckett's words to the priests just prior to his being murdered, in T. S. Eliot's drama, *Murder in the Cathedral*:

> You argue by results, as this world does
> To settle if an act be good or bad.
> You defer to the fact. For every life and every act
> Consequence of good and evil can be shown.
> And as in time results of many deeds are blended
> So good and evil in the end become confounded.
> It is not in time that my death shall be known;

It is out of time that my decision is taken
If you call that decision
To which my whole being gives entire consent.[61]

At deeper levels for every life and every act, as Eliot's Beckett says, consequences of both good and evil can be shown if one judges every life and every act by their consequences or results.[62] Beckett, the saint, has made a decision—if one calls that a decision to which this entire being gives consent—a decision that is not just in time but somehow also out of time. Time has pertinence to narrative decisions and moral choices, because moral decisions are made in time within the linearity of a temporal sequence, a sequence with closure bounded by time. Can we imagine a mode of being human which involves narrative decisions—a way of living in story— that might be nonmoralizing, and be not only in time but also out of time? I suggest that the mode of being human inaugurated by Jesus does not receive its coherence from bounded time and cannot be judged by its results. If closure and bounded time do not lend coherence to this way of living in story, what is its principle of coherence? What do Jesus' parables tell us are the truth and coherence intrinsic to a life lived in unending story?

3

Did Jesus
Tell True Stories?

Bounded Time

NOVELISTS AND film makers know well how to exploit our
willingness to suspend disbelief in the face of a claim to be representing historical events and characters. I began an under-
graduate course, "Jesus and Interpretation," by having the stu-
dents read Umberto Eco's novel, *The Name of the Rose.*[1] Only a
few of them could see through the rhetorical devices at the beginning of the novel. Most took literally the authoritative ma-
chinery that presents the text as one discovered and translated
from historical fiction, and they found it difficult, at least ini-
tially, to ask in what other ways the novel might have a bearing

on the truth. History is true, but fiction is not worth the attention of serious-minded people. In our culture, we have an extreme prejudice in favor of history (the bounded time of the
past) as being true.

The roots of this prejudice can be traced very far back into
both the Greek and biblical traditions. Of course the biblical literature depends on historical narratives as the preferred way of
registering reality. This prejudice was shared by the Greeks,
who also believed that, since historical narrative tells the story
of events that have happened, that which is historical is true.
Mythological stories were also recognized as being true, prob-
ably because myth also purported to tell what in fact had happened. The crucial distinction for the Greeks then was between
what had in fact happened, and what was merely the invention
of someone's imagination.

Of all the stories I have collected from late Western antiquity,
there are only two groups that utilize invented stories: the fables generally attributed to Aesop, and legal cases composed for
use in disputation in the pagan schools of rhetoric. These legal
cases (*controversiae*, as they were known) of course made no
truth claims. They were written specifically without closure,
and without plot, and without ideology, in order to provoke debate. I will not discuss them here, since they do not bear on our
immediate subject, even though they provide the closest parallels in a certain way to the parables of Jesus.

With the exception of the fables and the *controversiae*, then,
all of the other Greek, Roman, and Jewish stories draw on historical and/or mythological events or characters. The rabbinic
story quoted in chapter 2 has as its main character a purportedly historical rabbi, Rabbi Eleazar ben Shammua. Seneca's
story about Pausanias and Philip draws its characters and events,
again, from history. In Ovid's *Metamorphoses*, all of the stories
dealing with helping strangers tell about characters and events
who are both mythological and in some cases thought to be historical—Latona and the Lycian peasants, Jupiter and Lycaon,

and Philemon and Baucis. This is the case with all the other Greek, Roman, and Jewish stories. The only fictional characters of all the stories I have collected are recognizably fabulous—talking lions and panthers, compassionate hedgehogs, and the like. There is not a single example of a realistic fictional character in all of the stories I have collected. It seems safe to conclude, then, that in all the storytelling of late Western antiquity, there was not a single case of a character or event that was both invented and true.

History and Fiction in the New Testament

THE NEW TESTAMENT literature, of course, shares the ancient identification of history with truth. Our Gospel narratives implicitly appeal to the preference for the historical as the assured means of representing the truth. One could distinguish a true narrative by a first criterion: if it told what had happened, that is, if the events were "historical." And there was a second criterion: if the events of the narrative had been predicted by ancient oracles.[2] For example, I Cor 15:1-11 contains the earliest first example of "gospel," as it was preached by the earliest Christians. We have here the rudiments of a story—past events told in temporal sequence: Christ died, was buried, and was raised. Moreover, Paul says, these events occurred "in accordance with the Scriptures," that is, they are true not only because they occurred in the past but also because their occurrence had been predicted by the ancient oracles. This second criterion for recognizing a true event is to my knowledge evidenced elsewhere in the ancient world only in the pesher commentaries of Qumran.

Our modern criteria for recognizing the truth are not identical with those of the New Testament authors. Only certain fundamentalists are more likely to believe that something Jesus is reported to have said or done in the gospels and which was "predicted" by the scriptures is more likely than not to have really occurred. For example, in John 19:28 when Jesus says, "I thirst," the evangelist claims that this was said to fulfill the Scriptures (Ps 22:18). He makes a similar claim regarding the outpouring of blood and water when a soldier pierces Jesus' side with a spear (John 19:34-37; cf. Exod 12:46 and Zech 12:10). Today, using modern criteria, we are more likely to be suspicious of the account when something is reported to have occurred "in fulfillment" of the Scripture, because we do not share this ancient criterion of truth. For us, the truth of the New Testament is only bound up with the first criterion, with its implicit claim to tell what really happened.

JESUS TOLD FICTION, NOT LIES

ALL MYTHOLOGICAL and historical narratives, whether Greek or Roman, Jewish or early Christian, then, share the claim that the characters and events of the stories they tell existed independently of and prior to the narrator. The narrator implicitly claims not to have invented the story; rather, he or she merely re-tells it. Given this universal equation of truth with history in the ancient world, and its continuing dominance in our own day, when we ask the question, "Did Jesus tell true stories?" we must answer, "No, he did not." His parables are not accounts of events that actually happened, nor do they represent characters who existed outside the parables. The events and characters are not historical, nor are they mythological. The parables are fiction, the inventions of Jesus' own imagination. It is our very difficult and challenging task to attempt to describe how it is that Jesus told fictions that might be grasped as nevertheless "true."

Before continuing, it should be noted that the evangelists attempted to rectify this apparent deficiency of Jesus' parables by recasting them in order to mask their fictional character. In Luke's version of the man going down the road who fell among robbers (10:30-37), Luke or his source has added references to the known public world; Jerusalem, Jericho, the priest and the Levite, and the Samaritan himself all create the illusion that the parable tells a story occurring in real, historical space and time.

A second way in which the evangelists recast the parables of the lost coin, the lost sheep, and the prodigal son. They are all rewritten and set into a context that makes them refer to Jesus' behavior in eating with tax collectors and repentant sinners. Since now they purportedly refer to historical characters and events, they are not recognized as fiction.

Third, in both Luke's and Matthew's versions of the man who once gave a dinner and invited guests (Luke 14:16-24; Matt 22: 1-14), the story is recast in order to refer proleptically to the Christian mission and the destruction of Jerusalem. The allegories carry with them the implicit claim that the story is true because it refers to future events in public space and time. Since these events are already in the past at the time of the narration of the Gospel, it can be verified that they have in fact occurred, that is, that the parable refers to historical events.

Fourth, Matthew's version of the householder who went out early in the morning to hire laborers for his vineyard foretells what will happen at the last judgement. Again, Matthew makes the story refer to events that will actually happen in the future, in this case at the end of history.

In sum, the earliest Christians expressed their conviction that Jesus' parables were true stories by adjusting them to the prevailing sense of what is true, that is, by disguising their fictional character and lending to them the authority of historicity. This same impulse is also evident in historical criticism of the parables, best exemplified in the work of C. H. Dodd, Joachim Jeremias, and Norman Perrin. The idea is to read the parables as the evangelists did, not as fictions but as references to the historical circumstances of Jesus' ministry. In recent years, of course, this way of reading the parables has fallen into disfavor by scholars who have begun to recognize their fictional (usually called "metaphorical") character.

THE HERMENEUTICAL PROBLEM

GEORGE STROUP relegates parables to the periphery in theology and Christian life because, as he asserts, they "have no necessary relation to historical events." He believes that "enormous problems emerge if one tries to correlate a faith based on the interpretation of historical events with a biblical genre that has no necessary relation to history.[3] Granted that Christian faith has developed as one based on the interpretation of historical events, the question remains whether "the" Christian faith had its origins in this genre which has no necessary relation to history. True, this possibility creates enormous theological problems, but it also creates enormous theological possibilities, for, as I hope to show, narrative fiction is a medium whose meaning can, perhaps more easily than any other vehicle of meaning, survive the passage of time. In other words, parables could provide a resolution from the hermeneutical problem because story has the power to transcend time.

If we consider for a moment the hermeneutical problem of how to bridge the gap between what Christian faith meant in the first century and what it might mean today, we see that several different solutions have been proposed.

The first is to move oneself backward in time and to become a first-century person, adopting, insofar as is possible today, the attitudes, ideas, and beliefs and of the earliest Christians; one travels back to the past over an ideological bridge. In this view, Jesus was the founder of Christianity, and our task is to become first-century Christians.

A second solution involves abandoning the attempt to become a first-century person because, it is claimed, the structures of human existence are everywhere and always the same. When confronted with the word of Christian preaching, one need not adopt discredited conceptions, but instead make a decision for or against dependence on God. This is the Bultmannian, neo-Pauline solution to the hermeneutical problem.

A third way is that of John Dominic Crossan. In this view, the factor of permanence is that force which eternally annihilates human efforts to construct structures of meaning in this world. Crossan's hermeneutical principle is death.

Each solution to the hermeneutical problem requires that some principle have permanent validity and spans the gap of time separating us from the first century. The first accords this permanence to beliefs, the second requires that there be permanent structures of human existence, and the last assumes that the force that governs human existence is eternally the same—death. But what if there are no permanently valid beliefs, if there are no universal structures of human existence, and if death is not God? If Christian faith had its basis and origin in the parables, then it would be possible that story—specifically, the stories Jesus fabricated—would carry meaning through time to us who live almost two thousand years after his death. The enormous theological task, then, would be to articulate how the parables could still communicate truth to us.

In Chapter 2 we reflected on the phenomenon that Jesus' parables lack closure; that is, they do not appeal to the almost universal sense in the West that there is moral order in reality. The parables, then, are nondidactic and nonmoralizing. In terms of the way we usually register reality in the West, they are not true because they do not communicate, either by their organization of events or by the focalization of any ideology, a sense of a prevailing moral order. This is in contrast to all other stories told in late Western antiquity. Furthermore, the parables tell of fictional characters and events rather than historical or mythological characters or events. The parables, then, are nondidactic, nonmoralizing, fictional narratives. But they are also realistic. How can a story be both fictional and realistic? By what coding procedures do we recognize Jesus' parables as being transparent to the real world, when in fact they utilize none of the coding procedures universally accepted in Western culture for recognizing reality?

This problem is sometimes raised, in the form of an objection, by the opponents of the criterion of dissimilarity. They ask, "If Jesus was dissimilar, then how was he understood?" I would like to entertain the hypothesis that Jesus' parables are utterly dissimilar from any other stories known in Hellenistic and Greco-Roman antiquity, including Rabbinic parables. This will allow me to pursue further the question of how they could communicate a vision of reality.

Jesus and the Emancipation of Moral Imagination

I WOULD LIKE TO stress an important point. E. H. Gombrich, in a now classic work, observed that, "The story of the gradual emancipation of conscious fiction from myth and moral parable has not yet been told."[4] This is the story I am attempting to relate, for my research has convinced me that Jesus was the first narrator in the West to tell nondidactic, nonmoralizing, fictional, realistic narratives. This discovery—or assertion, if you will—is extremely significant. It would mean that it was Jesus who first liberated the human imagination by communicating the truth about reality. (I trust that the importance and implications of this discovery will be felt by all who would consider the role of the artistic imagination in theological reflection.)

If the parables do not function to illustrate purportedly true ideas, and if they do not exhibit closure, as the Western sense of a moral world order demands, then in what sense are they realistic, in what sense do they obtain on the real?

CONVENTIONAL NARRATIVE AUTHORITY

WE CAN BEGIN BY considering the meaning of realism in narrative. How does a narrative convey the illusion of reality? Gombrich has studied the way in which mimetic illusion is created by painting. When we raise the question of mimetic illusion in narrative, however, we are not asking how the medium imitates the visible world, as Gombrich does with painting, for narrative utilizes language, and language cannot imitate anything other than language itself.[5]

Narrative cannot imitate the visible world. Nevertheless, narrators from Homer onward have depended on visual mimesis for convincing their audience that they are hearing reports of events as they really happened. The usual way of claiming to tell the truth in ancient Greek literature, as in modern narrative, is for the narrator to adopt the role of the eyewitness. By reporting what people and things really looked like, the narrator creates the illusion that he or she was there. His or her descriptions stimulate our imagination to visualize the scene enacted before us.[6]

Because Homer represents events and characters pictorially, modern readers have much less trouble suspending disbelief in reading the *Iliad* and the *Odyssey* than they do in reading the purportedly historical narratives in the Hebrew Bible. The biblical narrators depend solely on closure and ideology to convey the sense that their stories are true, whereas the Greek narrators learned at an early stage to utilize visual mimesis. In general, the New Testament narrators do not rely very much on pictorial effects for creating mimetic illusion, although such techniques are not absent from the New Testament narratives. There are vivid pictorial effects in the Gospel of John, which even explicitly claims at a crucial point to be the report of an eyewitness (John 19:35). Of all the New Testament narrators, Luke displays the greatest interest in visual effects (e.g., Luke 24, esp. v. 51; Acts 1:9). He seeks to convey the "truth" of what he narrates to an educated pagan audience, steeped in the conventions of illusionism (Luke 1:1-4; Acts 1:1-5).

Narrators utilizing the conventions of mimetic illusion are particularly prone to providing useless and contingent details.

The presence of such seemingly useless details in a narrative—
the young man who left his linen cloth and ran away naked, in
Mark's narrative of Jesus' arrest (14:51-52) is an example—tends
to create the illusion that the narrator was an eyewitness and is
not simply organizing the events from his or her own imagination.[7] Erich Auerbach, in *Mimesis: The Representation of Reality
in Western Literature*, provided a now-famous discussion of Homer's way of dealing with Odysseus' scar. Auerbach's claim that
the basic impulse of Homeric style is to represent phenomena in
fully visible, externalized form is undeniably true.[8]

When a narrator reports what things look like, including apparently useless details, then the impression is created that the
narration is an eyewitness report. This is credible because,
when the maximum amount of information is given, the narrator's own presence is minimalized.

I would now like to analyze why this is true about eyewitness
reports. The scene dominates, and the narrator as eyewitness al-
lows himself or herself to be governed by externals that show
themselves through the report.[9] The resulting anonymity of the
reporter is perhaps what heightens our willingness to accept the
reliability of the report. Not only journalists but also scholars
and scientists are quite familiar with this phenomenon; their
personalities recede in the presence of the "facts." We tend not
to trust the narratives of people whose value-schemes or judgments or personalities are available for questioning. The eyewitness, that is, the reliable narrator, is a minimal self.

JESUS' NARRATIVE AUTHORITY

ANOTHER WAY TO narrate events is called, in narrative theory,
diegetic narration. Whereas mimetic narration imitates by
showing, diegetic narration tells. It is remarkable that Jesus
never asks us to envisage the events he narrates nor does he describe what his characters look like. Instead he tells what his
characters do. Considering that his parables lack closure and

ideology, which are always present in biblical diegesis, it is all the more striking that Jesus does not assume the role of eyewitness in order to convey an illusion of realism. As narrator, he never abdicates the role of selecting and ordering reality. He never permits the scene to dominate; by implication, his own imagination remains in control of events, selecting and ordering them. If the eyewitness as narrator is a minimal self, passively reporting, then Jesus as narrator is a maximal self, actively selecting and ordering reality.

The kind of authority Jesus exercises is extremely rare. No other narrator, or artist for that matter, in all of late Western antiquity presumes to speak about what really is the case based only on his own imaginative capacity to select and to order reality. By contrast, the evangelists assumed roles that were more in keeping with ancient codes for registering reality. In the Gospels, the events are so dominant that the narrators disappear entirely into anonymity. Of course Christians have not always been as confident as the evangelists were that the truth of the events narrated was its own guarantee. The Gospels of John and Luke already reflect some concern regarding the question of authority. In subsequent centuries, names were attached to the Gospels, and still today a great deal of energy is spent in debating the question of authorship, as if by settling the question one might give to these narratives the sort of authority their own authors did not claim for themselves, for they depended on the authority of anonymity.

Gombrich observed that a necessary condition for creating the illusion of reality is not to convey false information.[10] This condition might well also apply to narrative, both fictional and historical, as well as to painting. There can always be disagreement about what events and people really look like, and perhaps it is because narrative cannot by its very nature show events or characters that Jesus simply tells about them.

But Jesus does show what narrative discourse can imitate faithfully—speech. In direct speech, we have the maximum of mimetic illusion that narrative is capable of conveying. Jesus never uses indirect speech. Using word count as a rough guide, half of Jesus' core phonodramatic parables use direct speech. In sum, Jesus' parables have the minimum of mimetic illusion when telling what characters have done, that is, when narrating events, but the maximum of mimetic illusion when showing what characters have said, that is, when narrating speech. The characters are, as it were, present before us as they speak. What bearing does this characteristic of Jesus' parables have on our discussion of closure?

Modes of Being Human in Time and Story

THE CONTEMPORARY DEBATE about the way reality is ordered revolves around the status of closure in narratives and in reality. The postmodernists and deconstructionists advocate living without any illusions, which to them means abandoning closure in narratives and in human living. Their program deconstructs all narratives in order to expose narrative and the type of human identity predicated on closure as untenable fictions. The only honest way to live, in their view, is to take one day at a time until the inevitable end. The postmodernists prefer the minimal story—in the picaresque or episodic mode—like that of the unjust steward or the prodigal son. Their preferred mode of being human is the demoralized one of the vagrant, pervert, or bum. This of course is not a new theory of what it means to be human. The slogan "Eat and drink, for tomorrow we die" was widely known in antiquity, and has frequently given rise to efforts to live without consequences. Umberto Eco's treatment of the *fraticelli* in *The Name of the Rose* belongs to this tradition and can be read, if you like, as a humorous commentary on the program of deconstructionists like Mark C. Taylor.

At the opposite extreme stands what I have called the pro-closure party, which advocates a return to the traditional patterns of identity based on plot. In their view, this is how reality is ordered. They prefer a narrative genre that shows a causal relation between events and that ends by clarifying who wins and who loses, who succeeds and who fails, who is rewarded and who punished. This strategy produces character, and its preferred mode of being human is the moral mode.

SEQUENTIAL TIME

BOTH PARTIES TAKE sequential temporality as fundamental to human existence. One party believes that the sequence is inherently meaningless, that events happen to people, and that death governs all sequences, which simply terminate. The other party believes that people are agents of their own actions, are responsible for the consquences of their actions, and that the whole system is guaranteed either by human consciousness which judges or by a divine consciousness which is the judge.

THE CORE PHONODRAMATIC PARABLES

WHAT DOES reflection on the parables of Jesus have to tell us about what it means to live in story? And what mode of being human do they represent?

First, I will address the problem of the absence of closure in the parables. Since they do not exhibit closure, how can we describe them as stories rather than simply as episodes? If the moralizing impulse does not lend formal unity to these parables, then what is their principle of coherence?

If we are willing to grant that the parables are stories, even though we cannot yet articulate how they do cohere, then we can perhaps gain some insight into what lends them coherence by asking the following questions: Why did Jesus tell a story about the householder who went out early in the morning to hire laborers for his vineyard, and not about the laborers? Why did he tell a story about the man who once gave a dinner and invited guests and not about the guests? Why did he tell a story about the rich man who had a steward and not about the steward? Why did he tell a story about the man who had two sons and not about his younger son or his elder son? Why did he tell the story about the man going down the road and not about the robbers, the passers-by, or the innkeeper?

I find it easiest to think about why the steward, the younger son, and elder son do not have their own stories. The elder son subordinates his activities to what he imagines to be his father's project of being a father. The elder son is a helper to his father rather than a central agent on his own behalf in the story. The younger son and the steward both live episodically, like postmodernists, taking one day at a time.

MOTIVATION AND AGENCY

IN NARRATIVE THEORY, actions are said to be "motivated" when the narrator provides explicitly or implicitly a causal explanation for the character's actions. In Jesus' parables, all the characters who do not have stories can give reasons for their actions. The steward tells why he has decided to defraud his master. The younger son tells why he will go home to his father. The elder son explains why he is angry at his father. The laborers tell why they murmur against the householder. The invited guests all offer putative reasons for not coming to dinner. We can even infer why those who passed by the man lying half-dead on the road did so—they were motivated by avoidance.

For the pro-closure party, the principle of coherence in human selves, that which confers identity, is, as Christopher Lasch says, "defined largely through a person's actions and the public record of those actions,"[11] that is, through a character's ability to give an account of herself or himself. The postmodernists would agree with this description of the sources of identity, but they would reject the positive value placed either on having a self or on the demand to give an account of ourselves. If Stroup were right that Christian identity is connected with the ability to explain and to give reasons why we are the way we are, then the unjust steward, the laborers in the vineyard, the prodigal son, and the invited guests should all be model Christians. And as a matter of historical fact, the Christian tradition does recognize the three of these stories respectively as "The Prodigal Son," "The Unjust Steward," and "The Laborers in the Vineyard," largely because these characters inform us why they do what they do and we the audience are in a position to evaluate and to judge their reasons. We can see that the steward and the prodigal son are motivated by calculating reason, the elder son by filial devotion, the invited guests by their preoccupations, the grumbling workers by envy, and those who passed by, by avoidance.

Yet what is striking about the parables is that the actions of the main characters are unmotivated. Neither the characters themselves nor the narrator inform us why the father divided his living between his two sons, ran to embrace his younger son, or neglected to invite his elder son to the celebration. Why did the rich man fire his steward? Why did the host order his servants to go out into the streets and bring back whomever they found? We will never know why the householder paid all of his laborers a day's wage. Nor will we ever know why the third man went to the man half-dead on the road, bound up his wounds, brought him to an inn on his own beast, cared for him, and then contracted with the innkeeper to continue caring for him. There are permanent gaps in the causality of the events of these stories, leaving the actions of the main charactes unmotivated from the point of view of their narration.

The fact that Jesus' characters are active catalysts of events— subjects of actions—is important. The householder acted to pay all his laborers the same wages. The rich man acted to order his steward to turn in his accounts. The man who had two sons acted to divide his living between his two sons, to run and embrace his younger son, and to order a banquet prepared. The

man who once gave a dinner and invited guests acted by send-
ing his servant to call those whom he had invited. And the third
man acted by going to the man who was lying half-dead at the
side of the road, binding up his wounds, setting him on his own
beast, bringing him to an inn, and caring for him.

In acting, they did not passively select from among a given set
of alternatives; they did not choose as it were a path already laid
out before them. Each acted in a way that opened up a set of
new possibilities for action and reaction by the other characters.
Each has set events in motion. What might have been is a per-
petual possibility in the world of the postmodernist, who
chooses everything at once. In the world of the parables, by
contrast, each active decision by the main character sets in motion a series of narratives and reactions by the other characters,
and the decision cannot be undone.

MULTILINEAR TIME AND THE PERSONAL MODE

UNTIL NOW, our thinking in response to the parables has been
relatively straightforward. Now matters become much more difficult. The parables themselves are difficult to understand, and
still more difficult to articulate conceptually, not only because
they are parables, but also because it is difficult to find assistance when so few others besides Jesus have made the attempt to
verbalize this dimension of experience. In what follows, I have
found T. S. Eliot's *Four Quartets* to be the most helpful spring-
board for reflection.

Close analysis of the parables shows that the main and subsidiary characters each act in their own temporal sequence of
events. These sequences parallel one another. That is, characters do not live in a cause-and-effect chain of linear events;
rather, each lives in his own sequence. There are several temporal sequences in each story.

This is an unusual structural feature of Jesus' parables. Since
narrative employs language, and language evolves in linear se-

quence, stories always deploy events in linear sequence. "Story" time, however, is an abstraction, because real time, the time in which we live, is multilinear.[12] Story time, by definition, assumes away or subordinates the temporal sequences of subsidiary characters in order to achieve a linear sequence of cause and effect. Although this is especially true of plotted stories, even episodic stories focus primarily on the temporal sequence of a single character. That Jesus dissolves the abstraction of story time and builds his parables on "real," multilinear time can, I hope, be appreciated by considering the way his stories end.

At the end of the story of the "Householder Who Went Out Early in the Morning to Hire Laborers for His Vineyard" (Matt 20:1-15), it becomes clear that the workers have been evaluating the householder and that they expect him to act in a definite way in order to be the kind of employer they would like. They grumble because he does not fulfill their expectations. At the end of "The Man Who Had Two Sons" (Luke 15:11-32), it becomes clear that the elder son had expectations of his father, also, and he is angry at his father for fracturing the idea of fatherhood upon which the elder son had based his service and obedience all those years. The invited guests also objectivize their host, but in a different way. They all make excuses, showing that the host's offer of hospitality can be ignored. Each of the main characters suddenly becomes aware of that dimension where there are other selves. In these examples, the other selves are judging and evaluating, which is not surprising since they, as we have seen, are motivated: They know how to give an account of themselves to others and so expect others to do likewise.

One possible response by the main characters to the recognition that others expect them to give an account of themselves would be to insist on their immunity to approbation or reprobation, because, after all, they have done nothing wrong from a moralizing perspective. Such a response would involve in effect an insistence on the inviolability of one's own temporal sequence.

Instead, the householder wonders whether his own un-self-conscious actions might have provided the catalyst for the envy of the grumbling workers. The man who had two sons attempts to conciliate his elder son. The man who once gave a dinner and invited guests angrily orders his servant to bring back whomever he finds outside in the streets. What has happened?

In each story the main character has acted for a while in his own temporal sequence. But at the end of the story each of these characters is addressing a new, disconcerting situation brought about by the awareness that his own time is contingent with the sequence of another. What opens up here is the dimension of self and other. Previously the householder had ignored the workers' time, the father had ignored his elder son's time, and the host ignored his guests' time. Now, as each one speaks, each is aware of the time of others.

Time in the parables thus becomes quite complex—not the abstract linearity of stories but something like the multilinearity of real time. Here, perhaps, lives the realism of the parables and thus their claim to communicate the truth about reality! This moment is for each of the main characters, to paraphrase the words of Eliot's narrator in "Burnt Norton," a new and shocking valuation of all they have been,[13] for the pattern of their lives has been altered and has ceased to be a mere temporal sequence.

The voice of each makes the characters present to the maximum degree possible in narrative. Each is real in that sense. Moreover, each addresses a situation in which his previously closed temporal sequence has been brought into continguity with another temporal sequence and so opened up. In place of closure, ending, or finality, at the end of these stories we have opening and complexity, a sudden revelation of the genuine ambiguity that occurs when the consequences of actions are seen in terms of the way they penetrate the lives of others.

The act of speech is a communication between temporal sequences. The endings of Jesus' parables then record an illumination of the way temporal sequences interpenetrate one another. Since this interpenetration is not understood in a moralizing way, what Jesus conveys is an expanded sense of what it means to be a self. There is transformation onto a new level of being, where identity is constituted not by the law but by awareness of another's claims. This is what I have termed "the personal mode."

The most common narrative device for conferring individuality on a character is naming. The characters in Jesus' stories have no names, and yet we have no trouble recognizing them as particular individuals, distinct from one another and from ourselves. What is the principle of coherence in their stories? How is it that we recognize them as living in story when the usual codes—closure, self-identification through reprobation or approbation, and naming—are absent? Why is it not the case, as in the postmodernist program, that selves disappear, that the fundamental distinction between self and other is not obliterated but is, in some mysterious way, heightened?

Clearly, identity is not construed solely in terms of one's actions viewed as taking place in a solitary temporal sequence of causally connected events with specific outcomes.

Living in Unending Story

UNTIL THIS final moment, it is true, the main characters had acted as though unconscious of the time of others. But their final words indicate that they have, if only for this moment, broken out of their own temporal sequences and have focused their attention on the mutual embeddedness of their own temporality and that of others in the parabolic world. The parables end by disclosing that sphere of human being where our own temporal sequences are contingent on the temporal sequences of others.

The householder who went out early in the morning is, at the end of the parable, wondering whether his own spontaneous actions have been the catalyst for the envy of the laborers he hired early in the morning. The man who once gave a dinner and invited guests is ordering his servant to bring back those he happens to meet outside in the streets. The third man is incorporating the innkeeper into his program of helping the man who was beaten and left half-dead by the robbers. The man who had two sons is attempting to conciliate the anger of his elder son.

A passage from T.S. Eliot's "The Dry Salvages" illuminates the meaning of the way Jesus has concluded his parables:

> 'on whatever sphere of being
> The mind of man may be intent
> At the time of death'—that is the one action
> (And the time of death is every moment)
> Which shall fructify in the lives of others;
> And do not think of fruit of action.[14]

The mind of each character is intent on the sphere of being which can be called the interpersonal. Jesus as narrator does not permit us to think of the fruits of their actions, their outcomes; we are prevented from switching into the normal mode of approbation or reprobation. Instead of having an ending which permits judgment, the stories close with the speech of those who live in story, and their words show their minds to be intent on the question of how their actions have in the past fructified and shall in the future fructify in the lives of others. This, it seems to me, may be the principle of coherence for describing the particular, individually distinctive mode of existence (that is, the personal mode) as well as for describing what it means to live in parabolic story.

In Jesus' parables we see a mode of being human, neither that of those who live episodically nor that of those who live in moralizing plots. Both of these modes are imprisoned in time, in their own temporal sequences. Locked into one's own temporal sequence, the postmodernist descends into a mode of being that Eliot describes as:

> the perpetual solitude of
> Internal darkness, deprivation
> And destitution of all property,
> Desiccation of the world of sense,
> Evacuation of the world of fancy
> Inoperancy of the world of spirit.[15]

In contrast, those who live in stories of approbation and reprobation at least have the comfort that they judge as the world does, by results. If Jesus' parables provide our theological criteria, however, then in them we can see a new mode of being human that is neither nihilistic nor moralistic.

Jesus' characters transcend their own temporal sequences. In that sense, they are out of time. But they are also to some extent in time, the time of mutual temporality, of co-existence. Thus, time is conquered from within time by the sudden illumination wherein time past and time future are understood to intersect. This is the timeless moment, perhaps, of which Eliot speaks in the *Four Quartets*.

I would like to close by observing that there is a consistent relationship between Jesus' parables and his own story. Just as he did not allow endings, or death, to hold the key to the meaning of his characters' actions, so he did not allow his own death to hold the key to the meaning of his life. When asked to give an account of himself to Pilate, he refused; by his silence he refused to comply with the normal human need to judge actions by their results.

Of course, that does not prohibit those who argue by results from judging his life to be a failure because it ended in death. Geza Vermes, for one, concludes that Jesus' death was a "failure," a "disaster" turned into triumph only by the insinuation of the resurrection, a "happy ending" provided by his followers.[16] Even Christians sometimes tell the story this way. Yet from the point of view of one steeped in Jesus' parables, the resurrection is not a happy ending turning disaster into triumph, failure into success. Rather, in my view, the earliest Christians used their own culturally received concept of the resurrection appearances to reflect their conviction that Jesus' mode of being human could not be judged by its results, that death did not hold the key to the meaning of his mode of being human. Nor could death obliterate the meaning of his mode of being human. The clear implication of the resurrection experiences is that the personal mode is grounded in a reality which is ultimate, which engenders the lives of those who live in parabolic story. (This is, I think, the meaning of the doctrine of creation). The experience of the resurrection conveys the perception that death does not hold the key to the stories of those who live in the personal mode. Like the characters in his parables, Jesus lives in a story without end.

NOTES

CHAPTER 1

1. This observation cannot be reiterated frequently enough, it seems. The classic work by H. Richard Niebuhr, *Christ and Culture*, (1951; New York: Harper Torchbook, 1956), is still relevant. But in our time a better understanding of how the Christian movement originated from within Hellenistic culture is a desideratum for nonspecialists. For a comprehensive treatment, see Helmut Koester, *Introduction to the New Testament*, vol. 1: History, Culture, and Religion of the Hellenistic Age; vol. 2: History and Literature of Early Christianity (Philadelphia: Fortress; New York: de Gruyter, 1982). Also welcome are the various volumes in the *Library of Early Christianity*, edited by Wayne Meeks (Philadelphia: Westminster). The Hermeneia New Testament commentaries (Minneapolis: Fortress) incorporate a wealth of comparative material.

2. There are many different approaches to the question of what makes Christians or Christianity distinctive. The question, "What makes the identity of Christians distinctive?" is pursued by George W. Stroup in *The Promise of Narrative Theology* (1981; London: SCM, 1984), whereas Stephen Sykes investigates the question "What is Christianity?" in *The Identity of Christianity: Theologians and the Essence of Christianity from Schleiermacher to Barth* (London: SPCK, 1984). Both are symptomatic of the contemporary crisis of Christian identity. The subject matter pursued in *Jesus and Postmodernism*, in conventional theological language, is the doctrine of creation. That this is the case will, I hope, become apparent as these essays unfold.

3. *Ressentiment*, edited, with an introduction by Lewis A. Coser, trans. by William W. Holdheim (New York: Schocken Books, 1972) 43.

4. Ibid., 82, 105. I have given a fuller account of Scheler's arguments in *The Silence of Jesus: The Authentic Voice of the Historical Man* (Philadelphia: Fortress, 1983) 14-16.

5. For a useful, brief description of postmodernism, see Jean-Francois Lyotard, "Answering the Question: What Is Postmodernism?" translated by Regis Durand in *The Postmodern Condition: A Report on*

Knowledge (trans. Geoff Bennington and Brian Massumi; Minneapolis: University of Minnesota Press, 1984) 71-82.

6. Mark C. Taylor, *Erring: A Postmodern A/theology* (Chicago: University of Chicago Press, 1984) 6.

7. Ibid., 146, 23.

8. J. D. Crossan, *The Dark Interval: Towards a Theology of Story* (Niles, ILL.: Argus, 1975).

9. Taylor, *Erring*, 6, 15, 120, 121-48.

10. Ibid., 168.

11. Ibid., 162, 144, 162-63, 160, 168, 10, 14, 120, 161, 162-63, 152, 168, 166, 163, 10.

12. Ibid., 142-43. This is not a new phenomenon in the history of Christianity. Taylor's program appears identical to that of the *fraticelli* in Umberto Eco's historical novel, *The Name of the Rose*, trans. by Grappo Editoriale Fabbri-Bompiano (New York: Harcourt Brace Jovanovich, 1983).

13. John Dominic Crossan, *Finding Is the First Act: Trove Folktales and Jesus' Treasure Parable* (Philadelphia: Fortress, 1979) 113.

14. Crossan, *Dark Interval*, 37.

15. Crossan, *Finding Is the First Act*, 117.

16. The reversal of "good" and "bad" is diagrammed in John Dominic Crossan, *In Parables: The Challenge of the Historical Jesus* (New York: Harper & Row, 1973) 75. This moral reversal seems to be Crossan's primary concern, underlying all the other "reversals" he discusses in *Dark Interval*. For example: "one expects Jesus as a prophet of God to consort with the virtuous and not with sinners. If he does the opposite does this mean that the virtuous are sinners and the sinners virtuous, or what?" (*Dark Interval*, 92). See also pp. 102, 105, 107, and *Finding Is the First Act*, esp. 93 ("the Kingdom demands . . . the abandonment . . . of our *morals*." Emphasis his).

17. *Dark Interval*, 66-67, outlines his basic idea regarding reversal.

18. Ibid., 59, 60.

19. Sigmund Freud, "The Question of a *Weltanschauung*," in *New Introductory Lectures on Psychoanalysis*, vol. 2 of *The Pelican Freud Library* (trans. James Strachey; ed. James Strachey, assisted by Angela Richards; Harmondsworth: Penguin, 1973) 212.

20. Crossan, *Dark Interval*, 47.

21. Crossan confesses: "So for now at least, when I say that these stories (sc. the "master-stories" which distinguish art from science, claim that there is progress, or postulate an external reality) are not true, I mean no more than that they are no longer interesting. I am sure that if I were pushed to explain and defend the term 'interesting' I would say that the most 'interesting' story for me is that which best opens up the possibility of transcendental experience for here and now" (*Dark Interval*, 20; cf. 39).

Crossan thereby invokes the pleasure principle as a criterion of truth. Friedrich Nietzsche comments on this principle as follows: "It appears, if I have not misheard, that there exists among Christians a kind of criterion of truth called 'proof by potency.' 'Belief makes blessed: *therefore* it is true.' . . . The proof by 'pleasure' is a proof *of* pleasure—that is all; when on earth was it established that true judgements give more enjoyment than false ones and in accordance with a predetermined harmony, necessarily bring pleasant feeling in their train?—The experience of all severe, all profound intellects teaches *the reverse* ("The Anti-Christ," in *Twilight of the Idols and The Anti-Christ*, trans. with an introduction and commentary by R.J. Hollingdale (Harmondsworth: Penguin, 1968) 166-67; emphasis his.

In connection with Crossan's term "transcendental experience" (see text above, and *Dark Interval*, 20, 40-46, 57, 60, 122), one might also find apposite another of Freud's observations regarding "intellectual nihilism": "One often has an impression . . . that this nihilism is only a temporary attitude which is to be retained until . . . this task (sc., getting science out of the way) has been performed. Once science has been disposed of, the space may be filled by some kind of mysticism . . . ("The Question of a *Weltanschauung*," 212). As for the cogency of "intellectual nihilism," Freud observes: "All I can say is that the anarchist theory sounds wonderfully superior so long as it relates to opinions about abstract things; it breaks down with its first step into practical life. Now the actions of men are governed by their opinions, their knowledge; and it is the same scientific spirit that speculates about the structure of atoms or the origin of man and that plans the construction of a bridge capable of bearing a load. If what we believe were really a matter of indifference, if there were no such thing as knowledge distinguished among our opinions by corresponding to reality, we might build bridges just as well out of cardboard as out of stone. . . ." (Ibid., 213).

22. Werner Kelber, *The Oral and Written Gospel: The Hermeneutics of Speaking and Writing in the Synoptic Tradition, Mark, Paul and Q* (Philadelphia: Fortress, 1983) 73.

23. For further discussion of this verse, see Hans Conzelmann, *1 Corinthians: A Commentary on the First Epistle to the Corinthians* (trans. James W. Leitch, bibliography and references by James W. Dunkly, ed. George W. MacRae, S.J. Philadelphia: Fortress, 1975) 277-78.

24. (New York: Norton, 1984).

25. Ibid., 19.

26. Ibid., 29-34.

27. Ibid., 32, 52.

28. Ibid., 32.

29. Ibid., 18, 44, 59, 162.

30. Ibid., 57-58. In my opinion, the attitude of survivalism and thinking oneself a survivor (Ibid., 60-129) expresses the unconscious sense that death is ultimate. Lasch, of course, does not investigate the theological implications of his observations.

31. Ibid., 85, 96.

32. Ibid., 59.

33. Sigmund Freud, "The Themes of the Three Caskets," in *Arts and Literature: Jensen's Gadiva, Leonardo da Vinci, and other Works*, vol. 14 of *The Pelican Freud Library*, (trans. under the general editorship of James Strachey, ed. by Albert Dickson; Harmondsworth: Penguin, 1985) 245. A further observation should be made at this point. Nietzsche long ago expressed the opinion, in "The Anti-Christ," that the transcendent God of Christianity was "the expression of a profound discontent with the actual . . . " (*Twilight of the Idols and the Anti-Christ*, 125). Moreover: "The Christian's world of ideas contains nothing which so much as touches upon actuality: on the other hand, we have recognized in instinctive hatred *for* actuality the driving element, the only driving element in the roots of Christianity" (Ibid., 151). Again: "In God nothingness deified, the will to nothingness sanctified!" (Ibid., 128).

I do not expect that Nietzsche would have been surprised to find postmodernist "Christian" theologians deifying death. Whether postmodernist theology is the logical development of Christian attitudes identified by Nietzsche, or whether it simply represents the apothesis of the objective correlates of postmodernist attitudes, I must leave to cultural and theological historians to determine.

34. Stroup, *Promise of Narrative Theology*, 129-130.

35. Ibid., 14-38.

36. Ibid., 96, 171.

37. Ibid., esp. 175-85. On Augustine's idea of the introspective conscience, see Krister Stendahl, "The Apostle Paul and the Introspective Conscience of the West," *HTR* 56 (1963) 199-215; reprinted in idem, *Paul among Jews and Gentiles and Other Essays* (Philadelphia: Fortress, 1976) 78-96.

38. Frank Kermode, *Essays on Fiction: 1971-82* (London: Routledge Kegan Paul, 1983) 7.

39. Taylor, *Erring*, 14, 23, 68, 71. "The Drama of History stages the flight from death" (Ibid., 151).

40. Ibid., 15, 103-4, 108. As a commentary on Taylor's efforts to deconstruct and to negate traditional Christianity, Scheler's remarks on the apostate might prove illuminating: "An apostate is not a man who once in his life radically changes his deepest religious, political, legal, or philosophical convictions—even when this change is not continuous, but involves a sudden rupture. Even after his conversion, the true 'apostate' is not primarily committed to the positive contents of his new belief and to the realization of its aims. He is motivated by the struggle against the old belief and lives only for its negation. The apostate does not affirm his new convictions for their own sake, he is engaged in a continuous chain of acts of revenge against his own spiritual past. In reality he remains a captive of this past, and the new faith is merely a handy frame of reference for negating and rejecting the old" (*Ressentiment*, 66-67).

41. *Dark Interval*, 60.

42. Ibid., 122.

43. See above, n. 21.

44. In *The Silence of Jesus*, one of my aims was to examine Nietzsche's hypothesis that Jesus manifested "the psychology of the redeemer" ("The Anti-Christ," in *Twilight of the Idols and the Anti-Christ*, §§28-35, 140-48). Nietzsche based his interpretation on two "sayings"—"Resist not evil!" (Matt 5:39) and "The Kingdom of God

is within you (Luke 17:20) (Ibid., 141). The psychology of the redeemer represents a hedonistic form of love as felt where there is the "occurrence of retarded puberty" (Ibid., 144). The cultivation of peaceful, easy feelings can be sustained only by denial of any other. The psychology is virtually identical to that of the narrator in Margaret Atwood's *Surfacing* (Toronto: McClelland & Steward, 1972). The narrator says of herself as a young girl, that her imagination focussed only on "rabbits with their coloured egg horses, sun and moon orderly above the flat earth, summer always. I wanted everyone to be happy" (Ibid., 131). As she observes, "I must have been a hedonistic child" (Ibid., 91). To put Nietzsche's hypothesis to the test involved, first, identifying the authentic sayings and parables of Jesus and, second, reconstructing them. The interpretation of this core material disclosed that the evidence did not support Nietzsche's view of Jesus. Furthermore, the core material supplied criteria for determining whether "Christian" attitudes toward reality had their origins in "instinctive hatred of reality" ("The Anti-Christ," 142). My conclusion was that Scheler's arguments in defense of Christian love were essentially cogent.

45. It has become very fashionable to emphasize the "Jewishness" of Jesus, so much so that in a cover story in the *Atlantic Monthly* (vol. 258 no. 6 [December, 1986], 37-38), Collen Murphy asserts that "the fundamental fact about the young Jesus—indeed about Jesus at any age—is that he was, as Geza Vermes recently observed, 'a Jew and not a Christian,' " (Ibid., 51). Jesus' own statement, by contrast, is that he did not live as a Jew (Matt 11:16-19; Luke 7:31-34). See *The Silence of Jesus*, 22-28. Cf. Geza Vermes, *Jesus the Jew: A Historian's Reading of the Gospels* (1973; London: SCM, 1983), and idem, *Jesus and the World of Judaism* (London: SCM, 1983). More recently, with differences of emphasis, cf. E. P. Sanders, *Jesus and Judaism* (Philadelphia: Fortress, 1985); John Riches, *Jesus and the Transformation of Judaism* (1980, New York: Seabury, 1982) 105-6.

46. C. H. Dodd, *The Founder of Christianity* (New York: Macmillan, 1970).

47. For a representative recent statement, see Howard C. Kee, *Jesus in History: An Approach to the Study of the Gospels* (New York: Harcourt Brace Jovanovich, 1977).

48. This approach is articulated very clearly by A. E. Harvey in *Jesus and the Constraints of History* (Philadelphia: Westminster, 1982), and is explicitly adopted, e.g., by E. P. Sanders in *Jesus and Judaism*.

49. This empirical result lays to rest the claim that there was nothing unusual about Jesus' words (cf., above, n. 45). But it must be emphasized that the question regarding Jesus' "uniqueness" can only be asked, or answered, by faith. Nevertheless, there is a point of contract between historical-Jesus research and Christology. See, e.g., S. W. Sykes, "The Theology of the Humanity of Christ," in idem and J. P. Clayton, eds., *Christ, Faith and History: Cambridge Studies in Christology* (Cambridge: Cambridge University Press, 1972), 53-71: "If we deny that there is anything remarkable about Jesus, if Jesus really was an ordinary, fallible human being and no more, then our Christology has no basis in fact" (Ibid., 65).

50. Excellent examples can be found in M. Eugene Boring, *Sayings of the Risen Jesus* (SNTSMS 46; Cambridge: Cambridge University Press, 1982), and John Kloppenborg, *The Formation of Q: Trajectories in Ancient Wisdom Collections* (Philadelphia: Fortress, 1987).

51. I am using the narratological model constructed on the basis of the work of the best contemporary narrative theorists provided by Shlomith Rimmon-Kenan, in *Narrative Fiction: Contemporary Poetics* (New York: Methuem, 1983).

52. See, e.g., John Powell Clayton, "Is Jesus Necessary for Christology? An Antinomy in Tillich's Theological Method," in Sykes and Clayton, eds., *Christ, Faith and History*, 147-63, for the methodological issues.

53. Peter Camley, "The Poverty of Historical Scepticism," in Sykes and Clayton, eds., *Christ, Faith and History*, 171: "To claim objectivity and indeed, certainty in the accuracy of one's description of an object, does not mean that one must state everything that could be stated about it, but that one must have sufficient justification *for what one does assert*." According to the grounds that Camley gives (Ibid., 165-89) for claiming to know historical facts with certainty, an extremely high degree of probability amounting to certainty can be attached to the identification and reconstruction of the core material offered in *The Silence of Jesus*.

54. Hans-Georg Gadamer, *Truth and Method* (1960, London: Sheed & Ward, 1975) 333, developing R. G. Collingwood's idea. In-

cidentally, I am of course well aware of the hemeneutical questions raised by the employment of "scientific" methods described as steps one and two above, but have elected to set them aside in order to address more practical questions. In any case, I am not one of those who believes that our age suffers from an overemphasis on rationality.

55. In these essays I focus on the five "phonodramatic" parables, more commonly known as "The Prodigal Son", "The Good Samaritan," "The Great Feast," "The Laborers in the Vineyard," and "The Unjust Steward." See *The Silence of Jesus*, 100-214, for the evidence and arguments.

56. See above, no. 51.

57. (Philadelphia: Fortress, 1976).

58. Ibid., 39.

59. On "gaps," see Rimmon-Kenan, *Narrative Fiction*, 127-29.

60. Crossan, *Dark Interval*, 15-18.

61. Cf. E. H. Gombrich's comments on Cubism, in *Art and Illusion: A Study in the Psychology of Pictoral Representation* (1960; Bollingen Series 35, 5; Princeton: Princeton University Press, 1969) 281.

CHAPTER 2

1. *Complete Poems of Robert Frost* (New York: Holt, Rinehart, & Winston, 1949) 131.

2. Christopher Lasch, *The Minimal Self*, 36.

3. Ibid., 38.

4. Ibid.

5. *Jesus and the Constraints of History*, 71-72.

6. The phrase comes from Frank Kermode, *The Sense of an Ending* (London: Oxford University Press, 1967).

7. *Constraints of History*, 72. Interestingly, in support of these sentiments Harvey cites as an example "the experience of one who endured many months of solitary confinement in a German prison during the last war" (72). See Lasch, *Minimal Self*, 60-129, for evidence of how the concentration camp has come to serve as a metaphor of modern life, and, hence, as a rationale for adopting minimalist modes of being human.

8. The essay appears in Frank Kermode, *Essays on Fiction: 1971-82*, 133-55, and in W.J.T. Mitchell, ed., *On Narrative* (Chicago: University of Chicago Press, 1981) 79-97.

9. George Khairallah, "Our Latest Master of the Arts," *Academe* (Beirut, 1979), quoted in Kermode, *Essays on Fiction*, 133.

10. Kermode makes the same point about "Uncle Willie" in the "prologue" to *Essays on Fiction*, 8-32: "Uncle Willie" represents those who want to consume simple stories (12), who want the obvious and cannot grasp "the art of telling, this network woven of a succession of tiny touches" (9).

11. Trans. by Avital Ronell, in Mitchell, ed., *On Narrative*, 51-77.

12. Ibid., esp. 64-65: "The law demands a narrative account" (64). "The representatives of the law, those who demand of him an account in the name of the law . . . ; as a competent subject, he ought to be able to know how to piece together a story by saying 'I' and exactly how things happened to him" (64-65).

13. Ibid., 77. He takes this theme from the "recit" by Maurice Blanchot, "La Folie du Jour," which Derrida analyzes in the essay.

14. In Mitchell, ed., *On Narrative*, 1-23.

15. Ibid., 4.

16. Ibid., 13-14.

17. Ibid., 20.

18. Ibid.

19. Ibid., 23.

20. Ibid.

21. See Chapter 1, text at note 21.

22. George W. Stroup, *The Promise of Narrative Theology*, 91. Cf. also 87, 111-112.

23. Ibid., 91.

24. Ibid., 129-131: "Personal identity is an interpretation of personal history for the purpose, at least in part, of self-explanation" (129).

25. Ibid., 170-71, 175-185.

26. Ibid., 100-101.

27. See *The Silence of Jesus*, 105-7. Similarly, the prodigal son became a picaresque figure after liquidating his father's living; Ibid., 190-94.

28. Crossan for one would almost certainly deny this, even though he believes everyone lives in story. According to Crossan, the world does not exist independently. If everyone lives in story in the sense that everyone lives on rafts spun from their own imaginations, then the way is open for playing a variety of roles and assuming an endless variety of freely chosen identities. I use Lasch's concepts here (*The Minimal Self,* 32, 52) to characterize Crossan's views, which are explicitly directed against morality and in favor of play.

29. Paul Ricoeur, *Time and Narrative* (2 vols.; trans, Kathleen McLaughlin and David Pellhauer; Chicago: University of Chicago Press, 1984), 1.86.

30. Ibid., 1.5-30

31. Ibid., 1.31-51.

32. Ibid., 1.75, agreeing with Wilhelm Schapp. Cf. xi, 33. In the second volume Ricoeur argues for the primacy of narrative understanding.

33. Ibid., 1.75.

34. Ibid., 1.74: "We speak of a human life as a story in a nascent state."

35. Ibid., 1.59.

36. Ibid., 1.5-30.

37. Ibid., 1.31-51.

38. Although this point does not require demonstration, see John Onians, *Art and Thought in the Hellenistic Age: The Greek World View, 350-50 B.C.* (London: Thames & Hudson, 1979), for many interesting observations regarding the impact of Aristotle's ideas in the ancient world.

39. Ibid., 17.

40. Ibid.

41. Ibid., 16.

42. Ibid.

43. Ibid.

44. The research project, funded by the Social Sciences and Humanities Research Council of Canada, has surveyed all the extant literature from the Hellenistic and Graeco-Roman periods to collect all examples of brief narratives.

45. The narratological term for this is "focalization." See Rimmon-Kenan, *Narrative Fiction,* 71-85. The concept of focalization answers

the question, "Who sees?" but extends the visual sense to the cognitive, emotive, and most importantly, to the ideological orientation of the text. My interest here is primarily in the norms of the text - the "ideological forest."

46. Ovid *Metamorphoses* 6.315-81.

47. Ovid *Metamorphoses* 2.216-31.

48. Ovid *Metamorphoses* 7.620-724. See also Silius Italicus *Punica* 7.162-211; Pausanius *Description of Greece* 3.16.2-3; Plato *Phaedrus* App. 4.

49. One need only mention, e.g., that the Trojan War was fought because Paris violated the hospitality of his host Menelaus. In the *Odyssey*, the suitors of Penelope transgress the laws of hospitality repeatedly. Savages, like the Kyklopes, show no honor to strangers and do not mind the gods; they are rugged individualists: "each one dwells in his own mountain cave dealing out rough justice to wife and child, indifferent to what the others do" (Homer, *The Odyssey* [trans. Robert Fitzgerald; Anchor, 1963, 1961] book 9, 11.115-17, 265-77, pp. 148, 153). In the Hebrew Bible, there are, of course, the stories of Abraham and Lot's hospitality (Gen 18:1-8; 19:1-3) and of the old man's hospitality to a fellow Ephraimite (Judg 19:10-21). These stories illustrate that the obligation of hospitality was widespread. In the Abraham and Lot stories we find the same idea as in Ovid: You must extend hospitality to a stranger because he might be a god in disguise. Early Christian narratives about Jesus presuppose that he accepted the obligation of hospitality (esp. Mark 7:24, 14:3). Paul enjoined the Christians in Rome to "practice hospitality" (Rom 12:13), and the author of Hebrews advises: "Do not neglect to show hospitality to strangers, for thereby some have entertained angels unawares" (Heb 13:2). In the early second century the author of 1 Peter also advised: "Practice hospitality ungrudgingly to one another" (1 Pet 4). Cf. 2 John 10, where hospitality is not to be extended to a heretic. Also in 3 John 9-10: Diotrephes "denies hospitality to (itinerant) brethren, and not only that, he also prevents those who are willing from doing so, and excludes them from the congregation" (Rudolf Bultmann, *The Johannine Epistles: A Commentary on the Johannine Epistles* [trans. R. Philip O'Hara with Lane C. McGaughy and Robert W. Funk, ed. by Robert W. Funk; Philadelphia: Fortress, 1973] 101).

In Luke's version of "the man going down the road," Christian "love" was illustrated by the example of a Samaritan giving hospitality to a stranger (Luke 10:25-37). In this way the Christian conception of "love" was developed by adopting and transforming the ancient Mediterranean obligation to offer hospitality to strangers. "Love" was to apply also to enemies (Matt 5:43-48), as the law of hospitality did among the Bedouin (V. H. Kooy, "Hospitality," *IDB* (Nashville: Abingdon, 1962) 654.

Paul thought of Christian love as an obligation to "work for the good of all humanity" (Gal 6:10), an obligation which "serves also as a definition of Christian ethics." Hans Dieter Betz, *Galatians: A Commentary on Paul's Letter to the Churches in Galatia*, (Hermeneia; Philadelphia: Fortress, 1979) 310.

The dilemma caused by the appearance of a stranger at one's door is a familiar one to Christians in the helping professions—the conflicting claims of strangers in need and of family. Resentment is another danger. In humanitarianism, A (= family) is denied in order to affirm B (= the abstraction "humanity"). In tribalism, the endogamous breeding group (= A) is affirmed in order to deny the stranger (= B). Frost's poem, "Love and a Question" (*Complete Poems*, 9-10) strikes at the heart of the Christian dilemma because the claims of two concrete others are mutually exclusive:

> The bridegroom thought it little to give
>   A dole of bread, a purse,
> A heartfelt prayer for the poor of God,
>   Or for the rich a curse
> But whether or not a man is asked
>   To man the love of two
> by harboring woe in the bridal house,
>   The bridegroom wished he knew.

50. *Ecclesiastes Rabbah* 9.7.1.
51. *Ecclesiastes Rabbah* 11.1.1.
52. Seneca, *De Beneficiis* 4.37.
53. Lucian *Toxaris or Friendship* 19-21.
54. Lucian *Toxaris or Friendship* 43.
55. Aesop, from Plato *Phaedrus* 3.2.
56. Aristotle *Rhetoric* 2.20.6-8.

57. Aesop, quoted in Plato *Phaedrus* 4.9; cf. *Corpus Fabularum Ae-soppicarum*, ed. A. Hausrath, rev. H. Hunger (Leipzig: 1970).

58. E.g., "The Wolf and the Sheep," in Aesop, *Fables*, ed. Chambry (Paris: 1967) 231; "The Worker and the Snake," in ibid., 82; "The Ass and the Wolf," in ibid., 281; "The Traveler and the Satyr," in Avianus *Fabulae* 29.

59. *Gospel of Barnabas* 30.31a-b.

60. See Sir Richard Jebb, *The Oedipus Tyrannus of Sophocles* (Cambridge: Cambridge University Press, 1958) 157.

61. T. S. Eliot, "Murder in the Cathedral," in *The Complete Poems and Plays, 1919-1950* (New York: Harcourt Brace Jovanovich, 1952) 210-11.

62. Paul grasped this novel understanding of human life. Writing to his communities in Corinth and Galatia, Paul's concern is not with the meaning of actions judged by their results. A Christian knows that meat offered to idols is nothing and, judging as the world does, one might argue that the appropriate action would be to demonstrate one's new freedom from superstition or to do as one pleased (1 Cor 8-9). In Antioch, one could, as Peter did, think that one must not offend the sensibilities of Jewish Christians (Gal 2:11-21). On the surface Paul's positions seem contradictory in these two instances. But he can imagine how Gentile Christians would perceive the separation of Jewish Christians and almost imagine how those with weak consciences might perceive eating meat offered to idols. His ethical criterion is not what is "right" according to moral principles but according to how a Christian's actions might influence the perceptions of other Christians. He evaluates actions not by judging their results but by imagining how they might fructify in the lives of others.

CHAPTER 3

1. Umberto Eco, *The Name of the Rose*, tr. by Gruppo Editoriale Fabbri Bompiani (New York: Harcourt Brace Jovanovich, 1983). A recent film that employs the same device is "White Mischief."

2. On this point, see e.g., Frank Kermode, *The Genesis of Secrecy*, 102-123. On the pesher commentaries, cf. Michael E. Stone, *Scrip-*

tures, Sects and Visions: A Profile of Judaism from Ezra to the Jewish Revolts (Philadelphia: Fortress Press, 1980), 67, and Helmut Koester, *Introduction to the New Testament* vol. 1, 260-61. It is crucial to note that the principle of "proof from scripture" means, from the ancient perspective, that the ancient oracles (Scriptures) predicted the events!

3. Stroup, *The Promise of Narrative Theology*, 83-84.

4. E. H. Gombrich, *Art and Illusion: A Study in the Psychology of Pictorial Representation* (1960; Bollingen Series 35.5; Princeton University Press, 1969), 128.

5. Shlomith Rimmon-Kenan, *Narrative Fiction*, 108. The idea comes from Gerard Genette, *Narrative Discourse: An Essay in Method*, trans. by Jane E. Lewin (Ithaca, N.Y.: Cornell University Press, 1980) 164.

6. Cf. Gombrich, "Reflections on the Greek Revolution," in *Art and Illusion*, 116-45; and John Onians, "Allegory, Images, and Signs" in his *Art and Thought in the Hellenistic Age* 95-118.

7. Kermode, *The Genesis of Secrecy*, 54, 56, 102, 110.

8. Erich Auerbach, *Mimesis: The Representation of Reality in Western Literature*, tr. William Trask (Garden City: Doubleday, 1957) 4.

9. See Rimmon-Kenan, *Narrative Fiction*, 100-103, regarding the reliability of the "covert, extradiegetic narrator."

10. Gombrich, *Art and Illusion*, 90.

11. *The Minimal Self*, 32.

12. See Rimmon-Kenan, *Narrative Fiction*, 43-58, esp. 45.

13. "Burnt Norton," in "The Four Quartets," *The Complete Poems and Plays*, 125.

14. "The Dry Salvages," in *The Complete Poems and Plays*, 134.

15. "Burnt Norton," *The Complete Poems and Plays*, 120-21.

16. *Jesus and the World of Judaism* (London: SCM, 1983) 23.

Index of Names

Abraham, 89 n.49
Aesop, 51–52, 58, 90 n.55, 91 n.57
Alexander, 24
Aristotle, 40–41, 88 n.38
Atwood, Margaret, 84 n.44
Auerbach, Erich, 66, 92 n.8
Augustine, 38, 40, 83 n.37

Basthes, 50
Baucis, 44, 59
Beckett, Thomas, 55–56
Bedouin, 90 n.49
Betz, Hans Dieter, 90 n.49
Blanchot, Maurice, 87 n.13
Borges, 21
Boring, M. Eugene, 85 n.50
Breech, James, 7–9
Bultmann, Rudolf, 63, 89 n.49

Camley, Peter, 85 n.53
Clayton, John Powell, 85 nn. 49, 52, 53
Collingwood, R. G., 85 n.54
Constantine, 24
Conzelmann, Hans, 82 n.23
Coser, Lewis A., 79 n.3
Crossan, John Dominic, 16–18, 20–22, 29, 38, 63, 80 nn. 8, 13, 14, 15, 16, 20, 81 n.21, 86 n.60, 88 n.28

Damon, 49–50
Delos, 42
Derrida, Jacques, 36, 39, 87 n.13
Diotrephes, 89 n.49
Dodd, C. H., 23, 61, 84 n.46
Duke, James O., 9
Durand, Regis, 79 n.5

Earl, Edwin T., 8
Eco, Umberto, 57, 68, 80 n.12, 91 n.1
Eleazar ben Shammua, Rabbi, 45–46, 58
Eliot, T. S., 55–56, 72, 74, 76–77, 91 n.61
Esau, 45–46
Euthydicus of Chalcis, 48–50

Freud, Sigmund, 15, 18, 20, 80 n.10, 81 n.21, 82 n.33
Frost, Robert, 32, 90 n.49

Gadamer, Hans-Georg, 26, 85 n.54
Genette, Gerard, 92 n.5
Gombrich, E. H., 64–65, 67, 86 n.61, 92 nn. 4, 6, 10
Greimas, Algirdas, 28

Harvey, A. E., 34–36, 38, 40, 85 n.48, 86 n.7
Heidegger, Martin, 9
Hercules, 41
Homer, 65–66

Jebb, Sir Richard, 91 n.60
Jeremias, Joachim, 61
John the Baptist, 23
John the Evangelist, 43
Juno, 42
Jupiter, 43–44, 58

Kafka, Franz, 21
Kee, Howard C., 84 n.47
Kelber, Werner, 18–19, 29, 82 n.22

Kermode, Frank, 21, 35–36,
    83 n.38, 86 n.6, 87 nn. 8, 9, 10,
    91 n.2, 92 n.7
Khairallah, George, 87 n.9
Kloppenborg, John, 85 n.50
Koester, Helmut, 79 n.1, 92 n.2
Kooy, V. H., 90 n.49
Kyklopes, 89 n.49

Lasch, Christopher, 19–20, 33–34,
    39, 70, 82 n.30, 86 nn. 2, 7,
    88 n.28
Latona, 42, 58
Lot, 89 n.49
Lucian, 50
Luke the Evangelist, 29, 60–61,
    90 n.49
Lycaon, 43–44, 58
Lyotard, Jean-Francois, 79 n.5

Matthew the Evangelist, 26, 61
Meeks, Wayne, 79 n.1
Menelaus, 89 n.49
Minesippus, 50
Mitchell, W. J. T., 87 nn. 8, 11, 14
Murphy, Collen, 84 n.45

Narcissus, 19
Niebuhr, H. Richard, 79 n.1
Nietzsche, Friedrich, 14–15, 23,
    81 n.21, 82 n.33, 83 nn. 33, 44,
    84 n.44

Odysseus, 66
Onians, John, 88 n.38, 92 n.6

Paris, 89 n.49
Patte, Daniel, 27–28
Paul the Apostle, 14, 19, 59, 89 n.49,
    90 n.49, 91 n.62
Pausanias, 48, 58

Penelope, 89 n.49
Perrin, Norman, 61
Peter the Apostle, 91 n.62
Philemon, 44, 59
Philip of Macedon, 47–48, 58
Pilate, Pontius, 77
Prodigal Son, 17, 20, 26, 61, 68, 70–
    71, 73, 76, 86 n.55, 87 n.27
Propp, Vladimir, 27

Riches, John, 84 n.45
Ricoeur, Paul, 39–40, 53,
    88 nn. 29, 32
Rimmon-Kenan, Shlomith, 85 n.51,
    86 n.59, 88 n.45, 92 nn. 5,
    9, 12

Samaritan, 26, 28, 41, 52–53, 60–
    61, 70–71, 76, 86 n.55, 90 n.49
Sanders, E. P., 84 n.45, 85 n.48
Schapp, Wilhelm, 88 n.32
Scheler, Max, 14, 23, 79 n.4, 83
    n.40, 84 n.44
Schweitzer, Albert, 7–9
Seneca, 47–48, 58
Simylus, 48–50
Stendahl, Krister, 83 n.37
Stone, Michael E., 91 n.2
Stroup, George W., 20–21, 38–39,
    53, 62, 70, 79 n.2, 83 n.34,
    87 n.22, 92 n.3
Sykes, Stephen, 79 n.2, 85 nn. 49,
    52, 53

Tahnah, Abba, 44
Taylor, Mark C., 15, 17, 19–21, 38–
    39, 54, 68, 80 nn. 6, 9, 12,
    83 nn. 39, 40
Tennyson, Alfred Lord, 15
Toxaris, 48, 50

Unjust Steward, 24, 68, 70–71,
   86 n.55

Vermes, Geza, 23, 77, 84 n.45

White, Hayden, 37–38, 53
Wittgenstein, Ludwig, 9

Index of Ancient Sources

Acts
   1:1–5, 65
   1:9, 65
Aeschylus
   Agamemnon, 54
Aesop
   Fables
      Ass and the Wolf, The, 91 n.58
      Panther and the Shepherd,
         The, 51
      Wolf and the Sheep, The,
         91 n.58
      Worker and the Snake, The,
         91 n.58
Ancient oracles, 59, 92 n.2
Aristotle
   Poetics, 40
   Rhetoric, 52, 90 n.56
Augustine
   Confessions, 21, 38, 40
Aurelius, Marcus
   Meditations, 15
Avianus
   Fabulae
      Traveler and the Satyr, The,
         91 n.58

Barnabas, Gospel of, 53, 91 n.59

Controversiae, 58
1 Corinthians
   8–9, 91 n.62
   15:1–11, 59
   15:32, 19

Deuteronomy 23:4–8, 46

Ecclesiastes, 15
Ecclesiastes Rabbah, 90 nn. 50, 51
Exodus 12:46, 60

Galatians
   2:11–21, 91 n.62
   6:10, 90 n.49
Genesis
   18:1–8, 89 n.49
   19:1–3, 89 n.49
Gilgamesh, 15

Hebrews, 13:2, 89 n.49
Homer
   Iliad, 15, 65
   Odyssey, 65, 89 n.49

John, 65, 67
   19:28, 60
   19:34–37, 60
   19:35, 65
2 John 10, 89 n.49
3 John 9–10, 89 n.49
Judges, 19:10–21, 89 n.49

Lucian
   Toxaris or Friendship,
      90 nn. 53, 54
Luke, 65, 67
   1:1–4, 65
   7:31–34, 84 n.45

10:25–37, 90 n.49
10:30–37, 52, 60–61
11:20, 27
14:16–24, 61
15:11–32, 73
17:20, 84 n.44
17:20b–21, 27
24:51, 65

Malachi 3:7, 20, 45

Mark
7:24, 89 n.49
14:3, 89 n.49
14:51–52, 66
Matthew
5:39, 83 n.44
5:43–48, 90 n.49
11:16–19, 84 n.45
12:18, 27
20:1–15, 69, 71, 73
22:1–14, 61

Ovid, 89 n.49
Metamorphoses, 42, 43, 58,
    89 nn. 46, 47, 48

Pausanius
Description of Greece, 89 n.48
1 Peter, 89 n.49
Plato
Phaedrus, 89 n.48, 90 n.55,
    91 n.57
Psalm 22:18, 60

Qumran
Pesher Commentaries, 59, 91 n.2

Romans 12:13, 89 n.49

Seneca
De Beneficiis, 90 n.52
Silius Italicus
Punica, 89 n.48
Sophocles
Oedipus Rex, 54

Wisdom of Solomon, 15

Xenophon
Memorabilia, 41

Zechariah 12:10, 60